My friend Dr. Thomas Hale has written one of the best missionary books I have ever read. I have been with him at Amp Pipal Hospital in the high hill country of central Nepal, and life in that exquisite Himalayan country is as exciting and as difficult as he says it is. Tom writes with refreshing honesty and complete candor, laying out the painful failures of a pioneer medical missionary, but also lifting our eyes to see the greatness of God as He moves in beautiful and unexpected ways in the lives of the Nepali people. Tom has exceptional writing abilities. His style is clear, fresh, funny, and moving. After reading this book you will want to visit Nepal. And you will certainly be stirred to pray for the Hales and the other workers of the United Mission.

—**Dr. James Montgomery Boice**, Pastor,
Tenth Presbyterian Church, Philadelphia

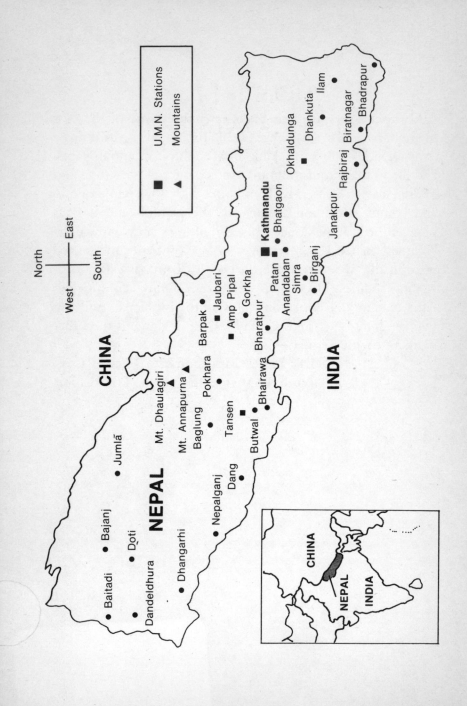

DON'T LET
THE GOATS EAT
THE LOQUAT TREES

A loquat tree is a small, evergreen, malaceous tree, native to China and Japan, but cultivated elsewhere for ornament and for its yellow, plumlike fruit.

—The Random House Dictionary
of the English Language

DON'T LET
THE GOATS EAT
THE LOQUAT TREES

Adventures of an American Surgeon
in Nepal

"When I give the signal,
everybody go
for a Loquat Tree."

Thomas Hale

Zondervan Books
Zondervan Publishing House
Grand Rapids, Michigan

DON'T LET THE GOATS
EAT THE LOQUAT TREES
Copyright © 1986 by Thomas Hale, Jr.

Zondervan Books are published by Zondervan Publishing House, 1415 Lake Drive,
S.E., Grand Rapids, Michigan 49506

Library of Congress Cataloging in Publication Data

Hale, Thomas, 1937–
  Don't let the goats eat the loquat trees.

  1. Hale, Thomas, 1937– . 2. Surgeons—United States—Biography. 3.
Missionaries, Medical—Nepal—Biography. I. Title.
RD27.35.H33A34 1986   617′.092′4 [B]   86-5648
ISBN 0-310-21301-0

Edited and designed by Julie Ackerman Link

Photo section: All photographs taken by Thomas Hale, Jr., unless otherwise
indicated.

Cover: Farmers plant living fences of pointsettias around their fields in an attempt to
keep their neighbors' goats from getting in and eating their crops.

Home Mission: International Service Fellowship, Box 418, Upper Darby, PA 19082

Field Mission: United Mission to Nepal, Box 126, Kathmandu, Nepal.

Unless otherwise indicated, Scripture is from the HOLY BIBLE: NEW INTERNA-
TIONAL VERSION (North American Edition), copyright © 1973, 1978, 1984 by
the International Bible Society. Used by permission of Zondervan Bible Publishers.

Printed in the United States of America

  90 91 92 93 / PP / 12 11 10

CONTENTS

PREFACE

When Cynthia and I and our two sons arrived in Kathmandu in July, 1970, we didn't expect the King of Nepal to greet us at the airport—and he didn't. But we might have been tempted to think how lucky Nepal was that we had come. After all, there couldn't have been many fully trained surgeons and pediatricians in that little kingdom of twelve million people. That attitude, however, would have been the worst we could have harbored. Indeed we had been warned of the harmfulness of such an attitude, warned that even a trace of superiority would create a barrier that would repel the friendliness and goodwill of any Nepali we met. All the same we found that rooting out our deep and often hidden feelings of superiority—feelings of importance, of being advantaged in background and education, of having so much to offer— was no easy task.

However as we became more and more aware of our own limitations and grew to appreciate the many exceptional characteristics and abilities of the Nepali people, not to mention the beauty of their land, we soon realized that we, not they, were the ones who were lucky we had come.

This book is a tale of our first twelve years in Nepal, of sadness and joy, of failure and success, and above all of Nepali friends and acquaintances. Since we have lived the entire time in the hills, the Nepalis most familiar to us are the common people—those who are uneducated, unpretentious, bound by age-old customs, and who, with dignity, are struggling against tremendous odds simply to survive. This book is about them and our life among them.

We draw a sharp distinction between these ordinary village people and the intellectual elite in Nepal, many with doctorates from our best Western universities who are competently building their nation and charting its future against nearly insurmountable difficulties. What is written here concerning the customs and conditions of the Nepali people does not apply to the growing minority of educated and enlightened Nepalis who are heroically leading their nation into the modern era. These men and women are among the most gifted and dedicated we have met anywhere. They are progressive and well-informed, and they know far better than most outsiders what Nepal's objectives should be and how to achieve them. Working with them and under them to bring one small area of Nepal the benefits of improved medical care and public health practices has been our privilege.

Nepal's leaders realize more than anyone the backwardness of the uneducated majority and their reluctance to accept new ideas. To surmount this difficulty, they have mobilized rural communities to support reform programs designed to improve basic living conditions. Much has been accomplished in education, health, agriculture, reforestation, and family planning. But for whatever has been accomplished, far more remains to be done. As fast as one problem is solved, another arises. Just maintaining achievements is an all-consuming struggle. Government ministers are frustrated by inadequate resources, by the lack of trained middle-level personnel to implement policies, and by the inertia of the impoverished majority, the main beneficiaries of their efforts.

Together with our colleagues in the United Mission to Nepal, we have joined hands with these Nepali leaders. In our various professional capacities we try, as opportunities arise and resources permit, to help alleviate suffering and promote education, economic well-being, and social justice. But we are asked repeatedly: Is our presence really welcomed in Nepal? How do Nepali leaders regard Christian missionaries working in their country?

The answers to these questions depend to some extent on who is answering. There is no question that the professional services of United Mission personnel are welcomed and appreciated. Our continued presence in the country is evidence of this. But since becoming a Christian is against the law in Nepal, the government cannot help but view the presence of Christian missionaries with ambivalence. Thus we have been invited to work in Nepal only under the condition that we do not "proselytize." This means that we agree not to persuade any Nepali to become a Christian by means of material inducement or other forms of external pressure. (This, of course, we would avoid doing in any case.) We are, however, free to practice our own religion, which includes making Christ known by word and deed.

The more conservative Nepalis, especially the Hindu priests, who still play an important part in formulating government policy, would prefer to place greater restrictions on our religious freedom. But more pragmatic Nepalis recognize that further restrictions would probably be unacceptable to the mission and would result in the loss of its services.

As a result both sides have chosen to work together in constructive harmony—each abiding by its own principles and each seeking to avoid unnecessary provocation of the other. There has never been anything secretive or deceptive about the operation of the United Mission. Consequently it has earned both the admiration and confidence of Nepali leaders.

Some may ask why we have come to Nepal if not to "proselytize" or "Christianize" the country. Our reason for coming, besides the fact that God has called us here, is to communicate the love of God to the Nepali people through our service and through our lives. We have come because God has given us a love for the people, especially for those suffering in body and spirit. This love does not arise from ourselves—it is a gift purely from God. Out of that love has grown a desire to introduce others to the person who has meant more to us than any other: Jesus Christ. To neglect sharing with our Nepali friends the joy of knowing Him would make a pretense of our friendship. To withhold from them this greatest gift would be to no longer love them. And so it is not our religion that we desire to introduce to them but Jesus Himself. There is no pressure, no enticement, no ulterior motive, no effort to undermine the many wonderful aspects of their own culture, which we not only admire but from which we have learned and profited. Rather we seek to work among the Nepalis as friends and equals, contributing our professional skills where needed and involving ourselves as much as possible in their national aspirations. During the course of all this, it is perfectly natural for us to share with them, as occasions arise, our hearts' deepest feelings. They can take Christ or leave Him; we shall serve them regardless.

The Road to Nepal

How do two American doctors, husband and wife, specialists in general surgery and pediatrics respectively, wind up working in a remote and exotic country like Nepal—and loving it?

The story of our adventures in Nepal begins in April, 1954. I was a junior at Phillips Academy in Andover, Massachusetts, headed for a career in politics. Together with the rest of my classmates, I dreamed of making a place for myself in the ranks of those who were to forge a new and better world. Happily unaware of my deficiencies and little inclined toward introspection, I fancied myself more religious and upright than most of my classmates. If anyone had asked me at the time if I was a Christian, I would have bemusedly answered yes, wondering less at the meaning of the question than at the absurdity of addressing it to me.

In that year something happened that radically changed the direction of my life. Gradually there began to grow upon me an awareness of a spiritual being apart from my own self-centered life. I was "Christian" enough to vaguely identify the object of this new perception with something I had always referred to as "god"—a god, however, that was for me more a concept to be acknowledged than a person to be encountered. It was like waking up in the morning and slowly realizing that someone is in the room with you, someone bigger than you—and what's more, he'd been there all night. For me it was an awakening to the presence of an all-powerful Creator who had made me, and now, in return, was demanding my allegiance, my service, my very life. I began to see not only the hollowness of all I valued and the selfishness of my ambitions, but also to sense the displeasure with which God must be looking upon my life. To have everything I had ever lived for steadily reduced to shambles was a deeply distressing experience. I felt emptied and unworthy; a sense of God's judgment hung over me. So real and overpowering was my consciousness of God that in the end, after an intense but short-lived struggle, I simply let go and turned my life over to Him. That was all I could do. That was all He wanted.

At the center of my spiritual awakening was the realization that there was nothing in me that was pleasing to God, nothing I could do that would be anything other than just one more spasm of self-centeredness. There was nothing I could offer that would stand His scrutiny. I learned, not without pain, that God could not build a new life on the site until the old life had been cleared away. It was just as Paul had said: "If anyone is in Christ, he is a new creation; the old has gone, the new has come."

No human agency took part in my conversion. I didn't know a single Christian personally, and I had read nothing that might have drawn me into such an experience. I was unfamiliar with the Bible. Consequently, when my former life was stripped away, I was left with nothing to hold on to—no book, no person, no church, not even a philosophy. In that vacuum God met me. Even today I can say that nothing so real, so certain, so compelling, has ever happened to me as that first meeting with God. I knew that God was enough for me, that indeed He was everything. So I cast myself upon Him—that's the one thing I did; and He honored it. And a peace and joy entered my heart such as I had never before experienced or even thought possible.

In those first few days God, in a supernatural way, made two further truths known to me: first, that He loved me and therefore I was to love Him; and second, that His love was embodied in the person of Jesus Christ, upon whose life I was to model my own. Thus I turned to the Bible, in particular the New Testament, to discover the substance of my new faith and the direction of my life. I was amazed at how true the Bible was to my own experience, and how authentically and clearly it spoke to me. I remember being perplexed by the fact that no one around me seemed to have a clue about this new life the Bible was talking about—and here it was available to anyone for the asking. Why was a prize this precious so universally ignored? I felt like shaking my classmates by the collar and shouting at them: "I was just like you; I thought I had it all. I was blind, but now I see. I've found it; and you can find it too!"

I gave up my dream of becoming a famous political figure and asked God what He would have me do. I was disturbed by Jesus' statement to His disciples: "If anyone would come after me, he must deny himself and take up his cross and follow me." I didn't seem to be able to tone down that passage. It meant to me that if I was going to be a disciple of Jesus Christ I had to go all the way, to hold nothing back, to give my entire life to God. That was a tall order, as I've found out every day since.

I discovered the passage in which Jesus, looking over the multitude, said to His disciples, "The harvest is plentiful but the workers are few. Ask the Lord of the harvest, therefore, to send out workers into his harvest field." When I read those words, I said to myself, "He's talking to me." For me that passage, as much as any other, was the call to be a missionary, a laborer in the Lord's harvest.

But which harvest? Follow Christ where? Not a week had gone by when I came across a small brochure put out by the Methodist Board of World Missions describing a new field that had just opened up for the first time in history—the place was the hidden Himalayan kingdom of Nepal. It told of the desperate medical needs in this far-off land of which I had scarcely heard—except that it was the location of Mount Everest. It told of a land of ten million people with less than a hundred doctors, most of them inadequately trained. It told of a land with not one of the lowest, but *the* lowest standard of health in the whole world—the lowest number of doctors per population, the lowest number of hospital beds per population, the lowest average life expectancy of any nation—twenty-nine years. Here was a land of extremes, from the highest mountain in the world to the lowest level of health—and, incidentally, a land with the lowest percentage of Christians: zero. Being a creature of extremes myself, it was perhaps natural that I was intrigued with a land of extremes. Whatever the reason, I immediately associated the Lord's harvest with the country of Nepal, and the command of Jesus to love my neighbors as myself with the plight of the Nepali people. I resolved on the spot to become a medical missionary to Nepal.

The first few months after turning from a self-centered life to a Christ-centered life were among the most remarkable I have ever spent. I discovered that the Holy Spirit the Bible talks about was not only alive and well, but was residing under my shirt. There has never been another period in my life when I have learned so much to such a depth, or have been so happy, or, I might add, so holy. I can vividly recall the free afternoons spent wandering through the large bird sanctuary adjoining the Andover campus, singing hymns from the chapel hymnbook, my heart almost exploding with joy.

With the psalmist, I had tasted and seen that the Lord was good. One gnawing question remained though: why had it happened only to me? I still knew no other person who claimed to have had an experience like mine, except those in books, and I couldn't imagine why more people weren't jumping at the opportunity to become missionaries.

I didn't have long to wonder: I began to stop jumping myself. At first God seemed to grow distant and fade away; then my ardor cooled, and soon disappeared altogether. The greatest thing that had ever happened to me was over, finished, just like that; and I couldn't get it back, try as I might. At the very least it was embarrassing; at the most, it was devastating. But even though my religious adventure had come to an apparent end, the mark it left on me was not to be erased. God had cracked the hard nut of my egoism.

I entered a period of listlessness, spurred neither by love of self nor love of God. During this journey through the desert, I drifted from one diversion to another, committing the worst deeds of my life along the way. Looking back, I think it would have taken just one Christian friend to have spared me all those barren years, a friend who could have explained to me that although the religious feeling had gone, the reality had not; that the Christian life depends not on the Christian, but on Christ; and that our inability to lead a perfect life does not condemn us to lead a bad one. I had started out well, but had stumbled and fallen. I hadn't known that the point of the race was not to win, but to finish.

Over the years that followed, I never abandoned my resolve to become a medical missionary to Nepal. The flame may have flickered, but it did not go out. Sixteen years of preparation intervened between my call to the mission field and our actual departure for Nepal in July, 1970— college, medical school, five years of surgical residency, and finally, two years in the army. In addition, I got married, which was the high point of it all.

Ours was a romantic courtship. I met Cynthia over a cadaver in the anatomy laboratory during our first year in medical school. After a few silent, eye-watering weeks of pursuing various nerves and arteries here and there through our formalin-reeking cadaver, I ventured to ask her what she was going to do when she got her medical license. She looked up from the axilla (armpit) into which she had been digging and said she was going to be a medical missionary. "Oh," I mumbled, "isn't that a coincidence. . . ." And from that day on we were pretty much locked into formation. No other cadaver in the anatomy lab received more hours of tender loving dissection than ours. I have little recollection of the rest of the course.

It is altogether probable that if Cynthia had not also entertained this peculiar notion of becoming a missionary doctor, she would never have looked twice at me. An Armenian, born in Lebanon, she had come to America at the age of nine. Her father, Dr. D. A. Berberian, was a well-known parasitologist, and her mother, a person of refined taste and artistic ability. Cynthia graduated as the valedictorian of her high school class and was elected to the Phi Beta Kappa Honorary Society in college. She was headed for a promising career as a concert pianist, but gave it up when she became convinced that God was calling her to be a medical missionary. It wasn't that she had either despaired or wearied of success—she had much to give up and little ostensibly to gain by going to some strange place like Nepal—but she too had committed her life to God during her high school years, and she allowed neither the memory of past artistic and academic achievements nor the lure of future ones to weaken her determination to obey His will.

My own return from the spiritual desert began with my acquaintance with Cynthia. She was an angel sent by God. True, I had always thought angels had to be blondes, but no matter. God is not limited by conventions. Since that time, Cynthia has not only remained an angel and wife, but over the years has added the roles of correspondent, public relations officer, cultural ambassador, finance secretary, and home minister—not to mention mother and pediatrician. Oh well, at least she can't do surgery.

Several years before our departure for Nepal, I fully rededicated my life to Christ. I happened to be reading the book of Revelation, and there I discovered (or, better, rediscovered) these words addressed to the Christians in Ephesus: "I know your deeds, your hard work and your perseverance. . . . Yet I hold this against you: You have forsaken your first love. Remember the height from which you have fallen! Repent and do the things you did at first. If you do not repent, I will come to you and remove your lampstand from its place. . ." (Rev. 2:2–5). How I could have overlooked these verses for all those years I can't say, but I suddenly saw that God was giving me one last chance. And I took it. A few paragraphs further on, my eye rested on the well-known words of Jesus that had meant much to me years before: "Here I am! I stand at the door and knock. If anyone hears my voice and opens the door, I will come in and eat with him, and he with me" (Rev. 3:20). So I opened the door, and He came in. He had been waiting there all the time.

chapter one

Scrap Metal

A *FEW MONTHS* before I completed my duty as an
army surgeon, Cynthia and I began the hectic business
of outfitting ourselves for Nepal: sleeping bags, kerosene
heaters, step-down transformers, kitchenware, tools, refrigerator, washing machine, typewriter, a five-year supply of
clothes in increasing sizes for two growing boys (ages one and
four), five years of Christmas presents—everything, it
seemed, but a toilet seat. (Cynthia's mother would bring that
the following year.) Nothing was available in Kathmandu we
were told, and if it wasn't available there, we reasoned that it
certainly wouldn't be available anywhere else in Nepal. We
packed everything in large drums. For padding we crammed
rolls of toilet paper (which supposedly wasn't available in
Kathmandu either) into the empty spaces, two huge cartons
of it purchased at bargain rates from the army PX.

I can still recall the wide-eyed girl at the PX checkout
counter staring at our pile of goods, then at us, then back to
the pile. Why did we need eight different sizes of children's
shoes, all at one time? And enough toilet paper to last a
company of men six months? What were we going to do with
the stuff—go into the retail business? There were regulations
about that sort of thing. We explained that we were going to
a very remote area where these items weren't available, and
she told us there was no place so remote that it wouldn't have

a PX. We said we weren't going to be with the army, which only confirmed her suspicions that we were into something illegal—or that we at least were abusing the system.

Finally we were rescued by a senior clerk who had read in the bulletin of the base chapel about our going to Nepal. "No problem," he said cheerily, helping us carry our purchases outside. The toilet paper cartons were too big to fit inside our Volkswagen station wagon, so we had to tear them open in the parking lot and throw the rolls in one by one. We got everything home in just two trips.

Two months before our scheduled departure for Asia, a letter came from the United Mission to Nepal saying we had been assigned to a small fifteen-bed hospital located out in the hills, a day's journey from Kathmandu. The hospital was still under construction. There wasn't even a road to it. We would have to fly to a grass landing strip and then hike six miles up a mountain.

Cynthia was stunned. This was more than she had bargained for. Since we were both highly trained, certified specialists—Cynthia in pediatrics and I in general surgery—we had assumed we would be assigned to the big 125-bed mission hospital in Kathmandu. It was the second largest hospital in the country, located in a large palace once used by Nepal's ruling family. There we reasoned we would be able to put to use a good part of our training. But what were we going to do in a tiny, ill-equipped rural outpost?

The letter put an end to Cynthia's long-cherished visions of missionary life in Kathmandu: the open and tastefully furnished home; the opportunity to entertain educated and influential Nepalis—perhaps even royalty; the piano concerts; an elegant but not extravagant wardrobe; the chance to use her silver service (a wedding present as yet unused, saved especially for Kathmandu). After all, the upper classes needed

God as much as the poor. But suddenly all those visions were swept away and replaced by a crude mud-walled house, where our neighbors would be illiterate and unkempt hill people. Cynthia made her biggest adjustment to life in Nepal right then and there.

For me, on the other hand, the challenge of a pioneer situation and the chance to rough it held great appeal. But it created another problem: What was I going to do for surgical instruments? A surgeon is helpless without instruments, and I didn't own even a pair of forceps. Under normal circumstances, hospitals provide whatever equipment a surgeon needs, but certainly this tiny rural hospital wasn't going to provide any. I had spent the past twelve years learning to be a surgeon, and here I was being put in a place where I would be unable to do what I'd been trained for. I saw myself spending the rest of my professional career treating runny noses, colicky babies, worms, and the itch—all cases that paramedicals were perfectly competent to handle. Twelve years of training and experience down the drain.

And so Cynthia and I found ourselves chafing at what we later would recognize was our first lesson in missionary life: Be prepared for a comedown. Being asked to do something *other* than we were trained for was not what bothered us so much; it was being asked to do *less*. We learned what every missionary must sooner or later learn: If it's job satisfaction you expect, forget about being a missionary.

We were fortunate to have had our illusions dispelled before we reached Nepal: We would have enough to worry about when we got there without being upset over our work assignment. So reluctantly we came to terms with the apparent fact that God wanted us in a remote village and not in a big city, and Cynthia began, with much agonizing and little enthusiasm, to scratch from her long packing lists the scores of previously indispensable items we would now no longer need.

A couple days after receiving the disconcerting letter about our assignment, I was performing an operation at the base hospital when the scrub nurse handed me a clamp with stiff action. I returned it and asked for another.

"That one needs some oil," I said.

"Get rid of this clamp," the nurse said as she passed the offending instrument to an assistant.

Get rid of this clamp . . . the words echoed in my mind for the rest of the operation. Good grief, if *they* didn't want the clamp, I'd be happy to take it. After surgery I ventured into the office of the operating-room supervisor, an intimidating lieutenant colonel, and cautiously inquired about the fate of the stiff clamp.

"If it's just oil it needs, we oil it," she said, clipping her words as if giving an order. "If it's corroded or bent, we don't use it." There was an edge to her voice. Perhaps she thought I was complaining.

"Would you happen to have any corroded or bent instruments, just . . . lying around?"

"I suppose I might," she answered suspiciously. "What for?"

"I thought if you didn't need them, I might have use for them."

"Where?" she asked.

"In Nepal."

"Oh, so you're the one going to Nepal." At once her sharp manner relaxed. "Well, let me think. Where do I have that box?" After a pause she got up and motioned for me to follow her.

We went into another room lined with drawers and cupboards. After rummaging in two or three drawers, she picked out a small box that contained about a dozen variously crippled instruments. "Can you use any of these?" she asked, offering me the box to inspect.

They were pretty bad, but not wanting to appear ungrateful, I began to select those that were at least useable. I must have looked disappointed—though God knows I had no expectations—because after I had fingered these disabled veterans for a few minutes, she said, "I think I might have something else that would interest you." Whereupon she opened a closet door at the end of the room and dragged out a large carton.

When she opened the top, I could hardly believe my eyes. It was filled with bright, shiny instruments, hundreds and hundreds of them. I began to take them out one by one, like a child dipping into a Christmas stocking and wishing the bottom would never come. Together we laid them out in rows along the counter. Not one was bent or corroded. As far as I could tell, they were all new, or at least in perfect condition. We finished unloading the carton in silence. The counter was covered with instruments: whole sets of clamps, all sorts of forceps, scissors, needle holders, dissectors, osteotomes, rongeurs, retractors of all descriptions, plus a number of specialized instruments needed for certain operations. There was enough to make up a basic surgical set and more. As I began putting the instruments carefully back in the box, the operating-room supervisor disappeared again into the closet. "Yes, I thought there was another box in here," she called from behind the door. "Come and give me a hand."

This box was even bigger than the first and was difficult to drag out. It too was full: dozens of Kocher clamps, Criles, Kellys, right angle clamps, towel clips, Allises, Babcocks, Sawtells, suction tips, dilators, and many others—all new-looking and of the best quality. I was speechless. Even the lieutenant colonel seemed impressed by the extent of the largess she was about to authorize.

"Nothing here is defective," I said. "What's it doing in the closet?"

"Oh, you know how surgeons are. We get them coming through here one after the other; they only stay a year or two. So a new one comes, and right off he asks for some special clamp he's accustomed to using. I say we don't have it and to use some other clamp we do have that's just as good. No, he says he can't possibly get along without his special clamp; no other will do; he's come from one of the very best training programs in the country and he won't work with anything inferior that might jeopardize his results, and so on. So what do we do? We order his special clamp, not one or two of them but a dozen. The army doesn't order less than a dozen of anything. And what happens to those "inferior" clamps that we had probably ordered specially for some previous surgeon who said he couldn't get along without them? They go in this box."

"Extravagant," I murmured as I gazed on the several thousand dollars' worth of instruments laid out before me. "But how can you legally give away army equipment?"

"We'll call it obsolete," she suggested, "excess and obsolete. I think there's a provision somewhere for getting rid of it. I'll check at purchasing and let you know for sure in the morning."

Like two conspirators, we shoved the boxes back into the closet.

The next day the operating-room supervisor was almost as eager to see me as I was to see her. Yes, it was perfectly legal. The procedure to be followed was first to declare the instruments "excess and obsolete" and then to sell them to a local dealer as scrap metal. I would buy the instruments at the rate of $1.13 for a hundred pounds. Thanks to my profligate surgical predecessors, I bought the two cartons for $1.69.

That was only the beginning. The hospital purchasing officer turned out to be an enthusiastic supporter of many kinds of missionary endeavors. He reckoned that the hospital contained closets full of excess and obsolete equipment, and he was going to help find them. Members of all the different departments joined the hunt. We found manually operated cast-cutters in the orthopedic department (they'd started using electric saws years before), cautery machines in the gynecology clinic (they had more modern ones now), an older model six-hundred-dollar cystoscope in perfect condition from the urology department, bronchoscopes and laryngoscopes from the ENT clinic, oto-ophthalmoscopes from the outpatient department—all for $1.13 per hundred pounds.

The administrator of the hospital, a career-army colonel, gave his blessing. It was as if all were eager to expunge their collective guilt for years of wastefulness by emptying out their closets for the people of Nepal. At the same time, especially among the permanent hospital staff, there was such an abundance of good will and genuine concern for needy people that I was deeply moved. I felt both humbled and awed to be the means of conveying their kindness across the seas. In the end their kindness amounted to fifteen thousand dollars' worth of surgical equipment. For me personally it was a sign that God was going to enable me to set up a surgical program in the remote Himalayan foothills of Nepal.

During those last weeks, as Cynthia and I sorted through the piles of instruments, we became aware that much essential equipment was still to be obtained if I were to be adequately outfitted to treat the large variety of surgical conditions I was likely to encounter in Nepal. Each surgical subspecialty required scores of specialized instruments, and many of these

I did not have. Furthermore, among the instruments I had received, there were gaps; certain sizes in a set, for example, were missing. If God had arranged for part to be supplied, was it unreasonable to hope He would supply the whole?

Just at that time we received a letter from Stan Barnett, an old friend and fellow student from medical school days, who was an anesthesiologist at the huge Brooke Army Hospital in San Antonio, Texas. As I read his letter I suddenly thought, *If so much excess and obsolete equipment could be found at our small 150-bed hospital in Albuquerque, how much more might there be lying around a 1,000-bed hospital?*

With ill-concealed excitement, I called Stan that same day. I told him briefly about the instruments I had obtained, how it had all been done legally and without the usual entangling red tape. In fact they had even dispensed with the scrap-metal charade after the first two cartons and had simply given to us all the additional equipment they found.

I asked Stan if he would be willing to approach the person in charge of his operating room—just to inquire—on the offhand chance. . . . There was a pause at the other end of the line. Perhaps my friend was mentally sizing up his operating-room supervisor, envisioning the outcome of such an encounter. After a moment he said, "Yes, I'll be glad to. I haven't seen any unused instruments lying around here, but that doesn't mean they're not stashed away somewhere. This is a big place."

He promised to call me the next evening. I had said nothing to him about what instruments I had already received nor what I still lacked. In fact our sorting had not progressed far enough for us to even know what we had, much less what we needed. For me to have compiled a specific list of necessary instruments would have been impossible, especially when it came to the surgical subspecialties, because I didn't even know the names of most of those instruments. I would be happy to take whatever was available. If there were duplications and *I* ended up being the one with an "excess" of certain items (an unlikely eventuality), surely one of the four other mission hospitals in Nepal could use whatever I could not—a much better use of equipment than to leave it sitting in a closet.

When Stan called the next day, he could hardly control his excitement. He had gone to his operating-room supervisor, a prim, efficient colonel, and mentioned our needs. She listened courteously, but when he finished, she shook her head and said she didn't think it would be possible. Discouraged, Stan dropped the matter. Later, however, the colonel had come up to him and asked, "Where did you say your friends were going . . . the ones who need the instruments?"

"Nepal."

"Is this them?" She handed him the current issue of the *Army Times*. There, filling most of the front page, was a picture of Cynthia and me with Tommy and Christopher. The headline read: "Doctor Team Becomes Missionaries." Below the picture was the beginning of an article explaining our decision to go to Nepal.

"Why yes," Stan exclaimed, astonished. "That's them! When did this paper come?"

"Yesterday. I just saw it now. I think I'll be able to help your friends. I hadn't really understood what they were planning to do or why they needed the instruments. I think it's wonderful what they're doing. I'll be delighted to help. Tell them I'll have enough things to fill up their car."

And she did. When I arrived with Stan at the Brooke Army Hospital a month later, the operating-room supervisor greeted me warmly, left what she was doing, and led us into a large storeroom. Along the way she called to an orderly to bring some empty cartons. Inside the room, below the counters that ran along three of the walls, were rows of drawers, each labeled with a surgical subspecialty. Five drawers were labeled ophthalmology, three were neurosurgery, four were thoracic surgery, six were orthopedic surgery, and so on. Dumfounded, I watched her empty the drawers into the cartons. The instruments looked new, hardly used. Complete sets went into the boxes in handfuls. I tried to protest. It was too incredible. Was it right? How could she do this?

"Major Hale," she said to me, "I've been here twelve years, and we haven't used these instruments once. You should see the equipment we have at the other end of this floor. These instruments aren't even spares."

She had started to unload the ophthalmology drawers. I could stand it no longer.

"I don't do eye surgery. I don't even know how. I can't possibly use these instruments."

"Surely someone in Nepal can use them if you can't." Without even a momentary pause she proceeded to empty the second ophthalmology drawer.

My scruples kept pricking me. "Those eye instruments, they're in their original boxes. They're still sealed. They've never been opened."

"That's right." Third drawer.

I watched the thin little boxes, each containing a single delicate instrument for eye surgery, accumulate in the carton. The names on the boxes meant nothing to me, nor could I tell by looking at them what any were used for. I had never seen a single eye operation in all my years of training. I didn't even know if the United Mission to Nepal had an ophthalmologist who could use these things, or even if there were an ophthalmologist in all of Nepal.

When the operating-room supervisor finished, we had

stacked up ten medium-sized cartons full of instruments. She looked briefly around the room, spied a two-foot-high cylindrical carton, and added it to the pile.

"Needles," she said.

Thousands of surgical needles. I had not gotten a single needle from the hospital in Albuquerque. But I had gotten suture material, two large sacks of it. So here were the needles to go with the sutures.

The operating-room supervisor accepted my faltering words of thanks, quickly wished me luck, and was off down the corridor.

We loaded the cartons into Stan's car and drove back to his house. Only after we had begun to unload and reorganize all my acquisitions, however, did the truly amazing aspect of the day's experience become evident. As with the needles and sutures, we discovered virtually no overlap between the equipment obtained from the first hospital and that from the second. For example, from the hospital in Albuquerque, I had received an incomplete set of urethral dilators; from the hospital in San Antonio, the missing pieces to make a complete set. From Albuquerque, plates for orthopedic surgery; from San Antonio, the screws to attach the plates. The many essential pieces that were not supplied by the first hospital were almost all supplied by the second.

When the two collections were added together, I found myself completely outfitted for every kind of surgery I would conceivably be asked to perform. From a total of at least a thousand different varieties of instruments (including many sets of six to a dozen, making the total number of individual instruments more than four thousand), I lacked only three special items: a dermatome, a drill, and an amputation saw. These were donated to me by medical friends in Albany, New York, just before we left.

I wish I could say I had not asked specifically for those three items, but in fact, I did ask. Even after seeing what God had provided, I evidently did not have the faith to believe He could produce those last three instruments without coaching from me. Or perhaps I didn't dare ask Him to do something still more remarkable than He had already done. Yet the three were provided—however one wants to apportion the credit.

When Stan and I had finished loading the cartons of instruments into my car the next day, there was no room left for even one more small box. The operating-room supervisor, as she promised, had indeed filled our car. As I drove east I thanked God over and over for His help, for this sign that He had indeed called us, prepared us, and had now even equipped us for His work in Nepal.

For years Cynthia and I had been so eager to go to Nepal that at times we wondered if it was just our own idealism, our own desire for adventure, or our own intrigue with a fascinating country that was prompting us to go. We had actually prayed many times that God might shut the door to Nepal if our going was not truly in His will. Now we could no longer doubt: The door was indeed open, even to the practice of surgery.

Only after we had been in Nepal six months, however, were my qualms about the eye instruments finally laid to rest. There was an eye doctor with the United Mission, Dr. Jack Moody, but he was scheduled to leave Nepal permanently within a few months of our arrival. The only chance for me to learn anything about eye surgery would be if Dr. Moody could teach me before he left. This he agreed to do, so we arranged for him to conduct an eye camp at our small hospital out in the hills. Many patients with a wide variety of eye conditions came for the camp, including fifteen patients with cataracts. Dr. Moody did the first seven cataract operations, and I assisted. Then he helped me do the last eight, and I was launched as an "eye surgeon."

Since Dr. Moody had brought all his own equipment with him, I hadn't bothered to unpack any of the little boxes I had gotten from the ophthalmology drawer at the Brooke Army Hospital. So on the last evening he was with us, we went through my collection of eye instruments to learn the use of each. As we broke the seals and opened the cardboard containers one by one, Dr. Moody repeatedly exclaimed, "What a beautiful needle holder . . . what a beautiful pair of forceps . . . what beautiful iris scissors . . . these are the best you can buy. Any one of these tiny instruments can cost as much as eighty or a hundred dollars."

After he had inspected them all, he selected thirty instruments and laid them neatly together. "You have everything here you need to do cataracts—a set far superior to my own." He then reviewed with me the uses of all the remaining instruments, occasionally fondling one or another admiringly. I had all that was needed to treat every common eye problem I was likely to encounter. Like the Compleat Angler, I had become the "compleat" eye surgeon. I was fully equipped, minus only knowledge, experience, and skill. These would come later, with the passing years.

Amp Pipal

*W*E FIRST ARRIVED in Amp Pipal on October 10, 1970, my thirty-third birthday. For the previous two and a half months, we had been in language school in Kathmandu, and now on a four-day break from our studies, we were taking the opportunity to visit the project at Amp Pipal prior to taking up a permanent assignment there in December. We had looked forward to this visit with great anticipation. After being cooped up in Kathmandu, we were eager to get out into the unspoiled countryside. Above all, we were anxious to see the place that soon was to become our new home.

The day was brilliantly clear as we boarded the DC-3 at the Kathmandu airport. The monsoon rains had just ended, and the land was washed in a deep luxuriant green above which rose the towering snow-covered Himalayas, extending hundreds of miles east and west along Nepal's northern border. The thirty-minute, sixty-mile flight took us westward over the foothills. Out the plane's windows we could look across the scattered fluffs of white to rows of spectacular peaks glistening above the clouds. They looked even higher from the plane than they had from the ground.

The flight was over all too quickly. In no time, it seemed, we began to descend. I watched from the cockpit as our Nepali pilot steered the plane along the narrow valley cut by the murky grey Marsyandi River. Far ahead along the riverbank, I could make out a tiny airstrip lined with white-painted rocks. The altimeter read fifteen hundred feet. As we drew closer, I watched as several barefoot airport attendants ran out and drove off half a dozen buffalos that had been grazing on the landing strip. We overflew the runway once to give the animals time to move off, circled around, and finally bumped to a halt on the uneven grass. As we got out of the plane, four-year-old Tommy announced, "This isn't an airport, it's just a field."

True enough. A small whitewashed building by the edge of the runway served as ticket office and waiting area for the three flights each week. A line of thatched huts behind offered hot sweet tea, a rice meal, and a night's sleep on a straw mat. These were the "hotels" of the Nepali foothills.

The crowd of villagers that usually gathered to meet the planes and haggle for jobs carrying passengers' baggage was nowhere to be seen. A wrinkled, decrepit-looking woman clothed in tatters quickly latched on to two smartly dressed government officials who had just disembarked. Hoisting their luggage onto her back, she marched off behind them, bent almost double beneath the weight of her load. But no other carriers were around.

We had thought someone would be sent to meet us, but we saw no one. Since we did not know the way or even the language, it looked as if we might have an interesting time trying to negotiate the bewildering network of trails leading into the mountains in the direction of Amp Pipal, six miles away. And what were we to do about the thirty pounds of rapidly thawing meat we had brought with us to distribute among the twenty or so missionaries living in Amp Pipal, their month's quota? Not to mention our own two suitcases and two small boys, the younger of which, aged one and a half, would have to be carried.

As we stood on the airfield trying to gather together our luggage, as well as our wits, a woman who had just gotten off the plane approached us. Without smiling, she asked, "Do you know where you're going?" Her manner made us wonder if we had made a mistake in getting off the plane in such a remote place.

We told her we were going to Amp Pipal, that we were the new doctors assigned to the hospital there.

She seemed unimpressed. "Is there no one here to meet you, then? A fine thing. Well, you'll have trouble getting porters today; it's the most important Hindu festival of the whole year. I'm not surprised no one has come for you."

She was an American schoolteacher, we learned, an independent missionary who had been teaching in a nearby high school for many years. She was a slight, gaunt woman of about forty, with light, quick movements and the efficient manner of a schoolmistress. Dressed in plain clothing, with her hair drawn severely into a bun, she fit perfectly our conception of the rigorously Spartan and self-denying single woman missionary.

She looked over our baggage, calculating perhaps whether one porter could manage both suitcases. "What's that?" she asked, pointing to the leaking meat box.

"Meat," Cynthia told her.

"Meat? What for?"

"For the missionaries at Amp Pipal," Cynthia replied somewhat defensively.

"Well, you'll never find anyone to carry *that* today."

"But it will spoil," Cynthia said, never one to let anything go to waste.

"Well, it will have to spoil, then," said the schoolteacher. "Why do they need meat anyway?"

Her question evidently was rhetorical, because she did not

pursue the matter further. Instead she picked up one of our suitcases and motioned for us to follow her to the row of hotels. There, after making some inquiries, she found a young lad who seemed willing to be our guide to Amp Pipal and to carry one of the suitcases and the meat. The other suitcase we could leave for someone to bring up the next day.

We bought some twine, tied the load together, and were all ready to go when the boy suddenly changed his mind. "*Najaane*," he said, indicating he would not go unless he received a bonus for working on a holiday. We were happy to pay whatever he asked. After all, what was an extra ten rupees (eighty cents) if it would get us up the mountain and save a hundred rupees' worth of meat?

But our missionary friend would hear nothing of it. "It would spoil the porter rate," she said. If one person paid extra, porters would begin demanding extra from everyone. That would hurt other Nepalis in the long run. "The missionaries may think they're putting a lot of money into the local economy," she said, "but they're causing prices to go up at the same time. A few get richer; the rest are worse off." It seemed useless to protest; she would not budge.

When it became apparent, however, that not only the meat but our whole family was going to be stranded at the airport, she decided *she* would carry one suitcase and take us to Amp Pipal herself, a journey many hours out of her way. But at that moment, another boy came along and offered to carry our things for us. We quickly struck a bargain satisfactory to all, and by half past one, only an hour behind schedule, we were on the trail north to Amp Pipal.

We had not walked twenty minutes when we met the porter who had been sent from Amp Pipal to meet us! He had gotten a late start because he had not wanted to miss the festivities in his village that morning. After a brief disagreement between the two porters, we agreed that the young boy should continue with us and the latecomer should go back to the airstrip and fetch the remaining suitcase.

Forty-five minutes later we came to the outskirts of a large village, and our carrier promptly disappeared. For a while we watched the villagers laughing and gossiping as they sauntered past: the women in gay velvet blouses of red, blue, and green, ears laden with gold, necks circled with colored beads; the men in clean pants and shirts. Both men and women wore their best clothes. Their foreheads were pebbled with rice that the village priest had daubed on with red and white paste in observance of the most holy Hindu day.

In some places, groups of women danced, and in other places, groups of men. At one end of a small clearing stood a crude wooden ferris wheel, its four double seats and eight howling riders revolving round and round at an incredible speed, considering that the whole contraption was kept in motion only by the feet of two young schoolteachers. Everyone in sight was having a thoroughly good time.

Except us. When our carrier had not returned after half an hour, we grew uneasy, then angry. Each minute of delay meant more walking after dark and increased the possibility that we might not get to Amp Pipal that day. Cynthia's humor was not improved by having to change Christopher's diapers to an audience of curious, giggling villagers who had never seen such a procedure before (Nepali children wear nothing below) and who were greatly surprised to discover that Christopher was a boy. Thereafter the onlookers showed more respect: It was a sign of blessing to have two sons.

Finally an older man, our carrier's uncle, came and said he would take us, but not until the next day. The trail was dangerous at night; there were ghosts, even wild animals. The little we could say in our garbled Nepali was clearly not going to change his mind.

As we sat wondering where we could spend the night, the Amp Pipal porter arrived from the airport with our other suitcase. With excessive courtesy he agreed to exchange loads and take us the entire way to Amp Pipal, even if we had to "walk all night." His determination, we soon discovered, had been fortified by some local holiday brew he had drunk at one of the many tea shops on his way to the airport. In any event at four in the afternoon, with five hours and five miles of walking ahead of us, we set out again with restored spirits. Tommy ran eagerly ahead along the trail, and Christopher, on my back, babbled happily at each new sight and sound.

The trail began to ascend through lush hardwood forests and across terraced paddies shimmering green with knee-high rice. Here and there large, dull brown birds watched us approach, then suddenly took flight to a safer perch, flashing at us brilliant underwings of iridescent blue. Once an entire tree fluttered to life with a raucous cackling as a hundred or more emerald-colored parakeets rose in a mass and skimmed off across the rice fields.

Gaining altitude, we watched the lower ridges fall away below us, their slopes dotted with thatched houses, scattered clumps of banana trees, and an occasional spreading pipal tree, a haven of shade for the tired traveler. Ahead rose Liglig Mountain, 4700 feet high and topped by three stone fortresses over four hundred years old, remnants from the time when Liglig was a tiny independent kingdom. The village of Amp Pipal lay on the opposite side of the mountain at 4000 feet. To reach it our path would take us up over a high shoulder, just skirting the summit, and onto the far side for the last fairly level mile of the journey.

As darkness descended the trail became steeper and rockier. We had not thought to bring flashlights, but a full moon gave us enough light to see the trail. Tommy rode drowsily on my shoulders; Christopher had long since fallen asleep in his kiddy-pack. After climbing for almost an hour over a particularly narrow, winding, and boulder-strewn stretch of trail, we spied two flashlights shining down at us from a high point on the trail above. Two of the missionaries from Amp Pipal had come to meet us—just in time: The moon was now hidden by the mountain, and soon after went behind clouds. We would have been unable to proceed ten yards without the flashlights of our friends.

Within an hour we had arrived at our destination. All that remained to be done, besides eating and falling into bed, was to feed our porter and pay him his wages. His load came to eighty-five pounds, which entitled him to ninety cents for his day's labor. It would have been twenty cents less on an ordinary day.

The sun was shining in the window when we awoke the next morning. We dressed quickly and went outside to see what kind of place we had come to. To the north, in stunning splendor rose the Himalayas, soaring to unreal heights above the thin wisps of cloud gathered partway up their lower slopes. The high peaks had been obscured by clouds ever since we had landed at the airstrip; now, after yesterday's trek, we had come to within twelve miles of them. We could hardly believe our eyes as we looked at the scene before us.

Immediately in front and on either side, the land dropped away into deep valleys 2500 feet below us. On the far side, leading up to the snows, ridge upon ridge rose in tiers, low and insignificant at first, then higher and more jagged, like the Rockies or Sierra Nevadas. Then came the snow line, and still higher, an imposing mound called Baudha, the nearest of the snow-capped mountains, taller than Mount McKinley. Above them all rose the highest peaks, which Nepalis believed were abodes of the gods, towering at elevations greater than

26,000 feet. We had to look twice to be sure they weren't clouds.

To the east and west as far as we could see ran the Himalayan foothills, heaped up in sharp and irregular folds. A few of the hills stood out prominently; like Liglig, they were sites of tiny independent kingdoms that existed before the nation of Nepal was born. Behind us the summit of Liglig itself rose precipitously five hundred feet, its steep northern exposure scored by deep gullies and sheer rock outcroppings. Near the top, patches of rhododendron forest nestled in protected coves; further down, the slopes were thinly wooded with a variety of semitropical trees, including species of wild cherry and wild plum. Near the bottom of Liglig's abrupt north face, two hundred feet below Amp Pipal and a mile away, lay the still incompleted hospital to which we had been assigned. Just a few minutes up from the hospital, but out of sight, was the little stone house that would soon be our new home.

The impressions of that first visit have not faded with the years. We wandered down endless paths, camera in hand, past flowering trees in white and purple, through mustard fields of gaudy yellow, across terraces pink with blooming buckwheat, along hedgerows of twelve-foot-tall poinsettias with scarlet involucra the size of serving platters. We passed clumps of giant bamboo, bending, creaking in the breeze, and watched groups of women singing and hoeing in their fields behind low stone walls. And everywhere we went we saw rice, rice, and more rice—then in its richest green, but soon to be gold for the harvest.

Except for the steepest slopes and the scattered patches of forest, every bit of land was terraced, planted, and luxuriant with growth. It wouldn't stay this way for long, though. Within six weeks the landscape would be brown and barren, and the mountains would be lost behind a veil of haze until the monsoon rains returned the following summer. But for then we were surrounded by a scene of such beauty and grandeur that it exceeded even our wildest imaginings.

Two months later we were in our new home. To transport all our belongings to the grass landing strip required one and a half planeloads. We were Americans, after all, and certainly any self-respecting American missionary ought to be able to fill up more than one DC-3. We had all those precious supplies bought in the army PX, enough to last five years, and drums of surgical instruments and hospital supplies, and the toilet paper. Our European colleagues graciously said nothing; I wonder what they thought.

Among our things was an upright piano that Cynthia, a former concert pianist, had purchased at a bargain in Kathmandu. For Cynthia coming to Nepal had meant giving up piano playing altogether, so she had not brought a single sheet of piano music. But God had provided a piano unexpectedly. Yet, in retrospect, quite expectedly, for isn't that the way God so often works: We give something up, and He gives it back. It was a good piano too, brought to Nepal years before by an official of one of the early U.S. government aid programs.

The piano came with the second planeload. It almost didn't make it; returning to Kathmandu, the plane developed engine trouble. After a long discussion as to whether the plane could be flown again that day, a mechanic settled the matter with a pair of pliers and a spool of wire. Some fittings in the left engine had worked loose, and when they had been wired securely together, the pilot was satisfied, and we took off with the second load.

Like ants attacking a crippled dragonfly, the villagers swarmed around the plane as it came to a stop. A DC-3 full of goods meant jobs for everyone, and they eagerly pressed through the door to select the loads that would most comfortably fit their backs. Their method of rolling our drums out the hatch without ramps made up in efficiency what it lacked in finesse. But when I saw them begin to push the piano into ten feet of empty space, I raced over, yelling and waving my arms, and just barely succeeded in averting disaster.

I had arranged with our project mail-runner (who eight months later would be sent to jail for murder) to hire ten men to carry the piano to Amp Pipal the next day. I figured they would know how to do it. After all, it was their livelihood. But when the next day came, they seemed to have no more idea how to carry a piano up a mountain than I had. They poked through the slats of the crate and pushed at the canvas above and below the keyboard, apparently wondering how something so hollow could be so heavy. They insisted it be dismantled before they moved it. Only grudgingly did they accept my statement that that was out of the question.

Several hours and a dozen half-witted suggestions later— some of them my own—we decided to tie four bamboo poles to the corners of the piano crate. Eight men would carry the poles on their shoulders, leaving two men in reserve to spell the others or to help in case of emergency. The poles were attached to the rectangular crate in such a way that the two rear men on the forward poles and the two forward men on the rear poles had to walk alongside the crate. That meant they would have to walk off the trail most of the way, because the trail was too narrow to accommodate both crate and carriers. Therefore, when the procession was finally underway and the momentum of the load began to move the carriers along of its own accord, the side men found themselves constantly being scraped through one obstacle after another—cactus fences, thickets of brush, jutting branches—or being forced entirely off the trail onto a lower terrace. This caused the entire crate to list precariously downhill and caused the men underneath to vigorously curse their incompetent counterparts at the other end of their poles. After two days of this jostling, the piano was in our house. Laurel and Hardy couldn't have done it better.

When we finally got the piano inside and had paid the men, Cynthia offered them some tea to drink and some liniment to rub on their bruised shoulders, which were unaccustomed to bamboo poles. Then she played "Claire de Lune" in appreciation for their efforts. They sat and stared, uncomprehending. For *this* they had lugged that crate two days up a mountain? But they were consoled by their wages, which were more than generous. And the deal was good for us too; the entire job cost only thirty dollars.

The piano, it turned out, had come to stay. A few years later an east-west motor road running seven to eight miles south of the airfield was completed, and plane service was gradually discontinued. From then on travelers had to cross one of several high, narrow suspension bridges, none of which could accommodate a wide load. Amp Pipal will always have a piano.

chapter three

New Doctor on Trial

*T*HE MEETING HAD BEEN CALLED for four o'clock, but angry men started arriving from all directions by midafternoon. Many had walked from great distances to participate in the proceedings. I could see them as they moved along the three main trails leading to the hospital. One trail wound up out of the deep valley 2500 feet below the hospital; another descended from the ridge above; the third, which I could see best of all, followed along the steep, thinly forested slopes of Liglig Mountain for more than a mile before disappearing around a bend to the south. This was the trail back down the mountain. It led past the police outpost, past the grass airstrip, and on to the town of Dumre, fifteen miles away. A few years later, the east-west road would come through Dumre. But in 1971, there was no road.

Even as the meeting was about to start, I could see stragglers hurrying along this third trail. The late afternoon sun highlighted their movements as they crossed the dark face of Liglig Mountain. The rest of the men were gathering on a flat stretch of ground just outside the hospital's main entrance.

Some were farmers who had come directly from their fields. They wore patched shirts and lengths of plain homespun cloth wrapped round and round in place of pants. Many were barefooted. Shopkeepers, schoolteachers, and *panchayat* (local government) officials wore mostly Western clothes. But all wore one thing in common: an expression of anger.

Murmurs of indignation rose louder and louder as the latest information passed between the small knots of men. These were not the phlegmatic, easy-going Nepalis described in books and orientation courses. Those who spoke gesticulated fiercely while their listeners grimly shook their heads. Some looked around menacingly; others spat. From time to time, oaths or shouts erupted above the sustained noise of voices. At other times the men seemed at odds with each other, hotly debating what should be done about the unprecedented happening that had brought them together. But one thing was certain: In the *cause* of their anger, they were united. The word was out: The new doctor had killed a cow. My own sense of participation in the proceedings was intense. I was the new doctor.

And this was Nepal, a Hindu kingdom, where to kill a cow was the same as to kill a man and drew the same penalty—eighteen years in prison—if the crowd didn't get you first.

Only a few hours before, I had been sitting quietly in my own house having a Nepali language lesson. It was a sunny mid-August day, a welcome change after weeks of monsoon mist and rain. The rich moist green of the hillside sparkled in the sunlight. Frogs and lizards feasted contentedly on the myriad buzzing insects brought to life by the warmth of the day. Birds chattered, foraged, and flew here and there, happy for the chance to dry their feathers.

After over thirty years of living in cities, this for us was the real life—close to the earth, nature unspoiled all around. Except for the hospital and its adjoining staff quarters a few hundred yards below our house, the mountainside was a scene of unblemished rural beauty. Living here was a form of emancipation for a city boy. Not a single day passed that I did not thank God for bringing us to this place.

Such were my thoughts that day as I sat laboring over Nepali grammar with my language teacher. Competing for my attention, however, was the beautiful Himalayan countryside that I could see through the window that overlooked our garden. It was only a small patch of vegetables, but it had cost Cynthia much labor and care as well as the salary of a gardener. But the garden was producing, so she considered the cost and effort worthwhile. And since it was our sole source of vegetables, Cynthia was determined to keep it producing.

There was only one problem. Our house had been built on a favorite grazing place for the livestock (mainly goats and buffalos, but a few cows as well) of neighboring villagers. I never consciously distinguished between cows and buffalos. To me they were all just large creatures with an endless capacity for eating.

For the past several months, we had tried to find ways to keep these animals out of our garden. Watching the product of three months of effort disappear in three seconds down the throat of one of those wretched beasts was simply unendurable. So we had finally built a crude but serviceable fence made of sticks and leaves and held together by strips of bamboo. When it was finished, I announced to Cynthia and a few of our colleagues that the animals could now come as they pleased; they could no longer bother me.

And they didn't—until that sunny day in August when, looking up from my Nepali grammar, I spied four large animals approaching the far end of the garden. *Thank goodness for fences,* I thought as I tried to refocus my attention on the lesson book. But the animals didn't move off. They had spotted Cynthia's giant cucumber vine growing exuberantly up the inside of the fence and, leaning over, had begun to yank at it. As the vine started to give way, I envisioned the whole fifty feet of it being consumed by these creatures—all from outside the fence.

I shouted to Cynthia that her cucumber vine was in danger and that she had better go out and do something about it quickly. Cynthia sprang into action. Running into the garden, she began hurling stones at the four beasts with unaccustomed vigor. But the animals continued munching, unfazed by Cynthia's exertions.

As I watched from inside, it struck me how futile her efforts were. For months before the fence was built, almost every day, I had seen her or the gardener rush out to chase away some animal. Today the owner of the animals wasn't even around; he had just let them wander as they pleased. They would come again tomorrow. And tomorrow. And tomorrow.

Suddenly I dashed out, vaguely deciding something different was needed. On my way I picked up the gardener's sharp-pointed sickle that was lying by the door, reasoning that if we put a little sting into our efforts maybe the animals would learn that there was some risk attached to roaming so near our garden. This reasoning, I'm afraid, attributed more intelligence to those dumb creatures than I myself was showing at that moment. In any event, completely forgetting that most of our garden was invulnerable, thanks to the fence, and forgetting as well that I did not care much for cucumbers anyway, I proceeded to drive them off, inflicting a small wound on the rear leg of one of them in the process. As they lumbered off, I returned to my language lesson, figuring that probably no one would even notice my efforts, much less learn anything from them.

I figured wrong on both counts.

About an hour later while still at my lesson, I heard a woman hollering a short distance away. People in Nepal don't have telephones; they don't need them. They just yell.

This woman had just discovered a cow lying in a pool of blood, and she was accusing five-year-old Tommy, who had just arrived on the scene, of trying to do the cow in. Tommy quickly set her straight as to who had done it, whereupon the distance her voice carried immediately tripled.

My language teacher, a courteous young Nepali, listened to the yelling woman for a few moments and then turned to me with a worried expression. "Did you do something to a cow when you ran out a while ago?"

A cow? So that was a cow. How dumb! I thought. Even grade-school children know that Hindus worship cows. They may not know anything else about Hinduism, but at least they know that. Certainly any missionary coming to a Hindu country is well aware of the need to treat all cows with utmost respect if he wants to endear himself to the people. I well understood this, you can be sure, but there is often a large gap between theoretical and practical knowledge.

We went outside and up the terraced fields behind our house. Others, attracted by the shouting woman whose voice had as yet shown no sign of tiring, were converging on the stricken cow. Some had discovered a trail of blood. Pointing and shouting excitedly, they followed it like men hot after treasure. As soon as we reached the scene, my worst fears were realized. I saw in an instant what had happened.

Midway down the cow's hind leg was an inch-long wound. I had cut a major artery located just beneath the skin behind the knee. The animal had managed to walk this far and then had collapsed for lack of blood. With increasing panic, I searched the cow for a sign of life. It looked dead and, judging from the amount of blood on the ground, it ought to have been. The Nepalis standing around certainly considered it dead. And so, to my despair, did I. The cow was motionless except for an occasional prolonged gasp. No more blood came from the wound, hardly an encouraging sign under the circumstances. I would have been thankful for any evidence of blood still left inside the animal.

By this time some of the Nepali hospital staff had arrived, including three young Christian men who belonged to our local church. Imagine their embarrassment. What a liability I had become to them. Whatever their feelings, however, they concealed them and quickly led me away from the increasingly hostile crowd. They urged me to stay out of sight for a while, which was advice I was more than happy to follow. Soon afterward the local government officials appeared, led by the *pradhan panch* (the town mayor). In view of the swelling outcry of the populace, he promptly agreed to call a general meeting to determine what should be done.

And so it was that within three hours of my misadventure, I found myself on that sunny stretch of ground outside the hospital entrance facing an angry crowd of two hundred villagers. I was about to learn what it really meant to worship the cow.

The pradhan panch attempted to call the meeting to order but abandoned the effort after a few minutes: The meeting had begun by itself. Eventually the men seated themselves and the hubbub diminished. One after another, each man rose to speak his mind. The long-standing enemies of the mission were quick to press their advantage, and for some time it seemed they might succeed in stirring up the crowd to violence. One man voiced his opposition to the mission by shouting, "First they take our land, then our water, then our firewood, and now they're killing our cows!" Another man, reflecting the viewpoint that cows were of greater value than humans, asked, "If he does this to a cow, what will he do to our children?"

Throughout the entire meeting, which lasted almost four

hours, not one word was mentioned about the benefit of our hospital to the community, nor was any appreciation expressed for the labors of the missionaries. At best, they regarded our medical work as a business proposition; at worst, as a means of enriching ourselves at their expense. Even those who knew we weren't trying to make money couldn't imagine that we had come to this place for *their* sakes; they figured that our motive for serving them was simply to gain merit for ourselves in order to improve our prospects in the next life. That was their motive for good works, and they assumed it was ours.

I spent the greater part of the meeting staring blankly ahead of me at the bobbing sea of multicolored topis (the national cap, worn by most of the men), trying to avoid the angry eyes that glared in my direction. My meager knowledge of the Nepali language, not to mention a certain dispossession of mind, prevented me from understanding most of what was happening. Two of our senior missionaries were present to speak if necessary for the mission, and from them I was able to piece together a general outline of the proceedings.

The crowd, it appeared, was divided over whether to report this matter to higher government officials in the district capital, a six-hour walk to the east, or whether to dispose of the matter themselves.

Some felt that if the case were referred to the district authorities, the local community would lose all chance to profit from the affair, meaning they would not be able to collect the enormous sum they hoped to extort from the rich "Americani" doctor as a reward for hushing things up. Others, equally vociferous, denounced such tactics and argued that it was unthinkable not to report such a major event as the murder of a cow, that it couldn't be hushed up for long anyway, and that once it did come to light, their entire panchayat would be disgraced and its officers dismissed. As for the mission, it was going to lose badly whichever side won.

In the heat of the debate, with no resolution in sight, someone thought to inquire about the condition of the cow. One of the Nepali Christians, who had just returned from checking on the animal, informed the assembly that the cow was indeed still alive, though barely so. Whereupon the pradhan panch, seeing his opportunity to bring the debate to a temporary conclusion, suggested that there was no point in deliberating further until it was known whether the cow would live or die. Primarily because of the lateness of the hour rather than because of any desire to oblige their pradhan panch, the men reluctantly agreed to break up for the day and to reassemble in the morning, by which time the fate of the cow would probably be settled one way or the other.

As dusk crept up the mountainside from the valley below, the crowd dispersed to their homes, a few of them lingering to shoot me one last menacing look before walking off into the fading light. Only four or five fellow missionaries and a few of our Nepali hospital staff remained behind. Everything now hung on each labored breath of the bloodless cow. No one spoke of the probability that the cow would die, but the prospect dominated our thoughts. Even if the animal survived, the penalty for merely injuring a cow was two years in prison.

I couldn't help recalling the story I'd recently heard about the mission ambulance driver in Kathmandu who managed to drive his ambulance into a cow. He had allegedly parked the vehicle and left it in a forward gear. When he returned from his business and started the motor, the Land Rover leaped forward into a cow that had, during the driver's absence, laid itself down to sleep by the front wheels. A throng quickly materialized, followed by some policemen. The cow was taken to the government animal hospital for observation, while the unfortunate ambulance driver was carted off to jail. He was released a few days later when it was determined the cow had sustained no injury.

One thing was sure: The mistreatment of a cow was not taken lightly in this land. Even if no injury were inflicted, just assaulting a cow was sufficient to net one a fine of two hundred rupees (about eighteen dollars). At least such were the interpretations of the law that were imparted to us by various panchayat officials during the course of the afternoon. Whether or not these interpretations actually corresponded to the written constitution, it appeared that they would be forming the basis of any judgment against me. I didn't feel in a position at that point to demand to know my constitutional rights. As far as I knew, there wasn't a lawyer in the district, except perhaps the prosecuting attorney.

But no matter what legal recourse might be found to minimize the eventual sentence, one thing seemed evident: The damage had already been done. My career in Amp Pipal and, most probably in Nepal, had come to a sudden and inglorious end.

We walked silently up the terraced hillside to where the cow still lay, motionless except for its slow, measured breathing. The tiny wound was still visible in the dim light. Someone suggested that I tie off the severed artery lest it begin to bleed again. Our Nepali lab technician thought some penicillin would help.

Since I was the only practicing doctor in Amp Pipal at the time, I pulled myself together and endured the added humiliation of repairing my own damage. The lab technician and my Nepali operating-room assistant, both members of our church, went down to the hospital to fetch a stretcher. In the last glow of twilight, we carried our special patient to an empty room in the tuberculosis ward. By the light of a kerosene lamp, with my anxious friends looking on, I tied off the artery and sutured the wound with, I might add, as much care as I have ever treated any wound in my life, before or since.

One of our Nepali nurses brought a quadruple dose of penicillin, while our builder, a fellow missionary from Ohio named Stan Kamp, sent one of his workmen to get some straw and water for the cow—though it hadn't the strength, much less the inclination, to even open its mouth.

Having done what we could to make the cow comfortable, we left it in the charge of Tej, the hospital laundryman, who was instructed to do his best to get the animal to eat and drink. The others went to their various houses and later to a prayer meeting where they prayed long and earnestly that the outcome to the day's events might somehow be favorable, that the cow might recover, and that God's honor might not be further tarnished. I retired alone to spend a very bad night.

Even though I knew that so large an animal could not die from so small a wound, try as I might I could not convince myself that it was true. All I could see was an end to a dream, an end to working in this place that suited us so perfectly and which we had come to love so much. Then there was the jeopardy into which I had placed the hospital and our entire project—the entire mission, for that matter. I remembered the beatitude about being persecuted for righteousness' sake and thought how easy that must be compared to suffering for stupidity's sake. After hours of profitless brooding, I finally dozed off to sleep shortly before dawn.

When I awoke, the sun was already shining on the distant snowy peaks to the west. But in front of them over the valley, a light rain was falling, and there, through the mist from horizon to horizon, extended the most brilliant double rainbow I had ever seen. Its inner ring was so vivid that I wanted to reach out and touch it. I was not surprised a few minutes later when the hospital cashier bounded up to the house to say the cow was fine and was actually standing up, eating, and drinking.

When I walked down to the hospital that morning to face the crowd again, I was at peace, both in mind and spirit.

Many more people had gathered outside the hospital than were there the day before, but the mood of the group was completely transformed. No hostile words for me or the mission were spoken; instead, the men were friendly and conciliatory. The emphasis was on the service the mission was providing, the ignorance of the doctor in matters of livestock identification and Nepali law, and the need for greater understanding of each other.

The entire affair probably would have been settled for a two-hundred-rupee fine—just to comply with the law, lest the panchayat later be accused of having overlooked a crime—except for one thing: The cow's owner was one of the most disreputable and avaricious men on the mountain and a confirmed opponent of the mission as well. Since there had never been a case like this in the entire district, no one knew how to handle it, though everyone had an opinion. Opposing political factions contended with one another, some groups hoping to use the incident to oust other groups. In the end, after two hours of heated debate, they agreed that I should pay damages to the owner of the cow in the form of a personal settlement. They assumed his demand would be reasonable—four to five hundred rupees.

But their estimate was low. He demanded twenty-five thousand rupees (twenty-two hundred dollars). Everyone but his family and close neighbors were disgusted by his demand

and began to shout at him with greater vehemence than they had exhibited during the entire morning. But he was as stubborn as a goat and was not about to lose this chance to enrich himself. For two more hours they tried to get his price down and argued that if the matter couldn't be settled locally it would have to be referred to the district capital and settled there. Neither we nor the cow owner particularly favored that alternative: The cow owner, because he would get only two hundred rupees; we, because we did not want the affair to spread any further than necessary.

After much bickering we agreed on a payment of two thousand rupees (one hundred and eighty dollars), an amount far greater than the average Nepali could earn in a year. Most of those present felt it was exorbitant. At the end of the meeting, the pradhan panch asked that I please not be angry with them over what had happened. Paying such a high price had one distinct advantage: It removed any lingering resentment that the crowd might otherwise have felt. Even the owner of the cow became most friendly and cheerful after the settlement.

For the next thirty-five days, with Tej for a private duty nurse and with as much tasty straw as it could eat, the cow occupied its own private room in the hospital. According to Nepali law, I would not be liable for what happened to the cow after that period of time.

The patient caused me no little anxiety in the beginning. It chewed off its dressing and pulled out my carefully placed stitches with its teeth, whereupon the wound gaped open and became infected. But then I realized that God gave cows tongues for purposes other than savoring cucumber vines: In no time the cow had licked the wound clean, and helped along by generous applications of cow manure and straw dust, it had healed completely by the end of the second week.

In the end that cow did much more for me than I did for it. It took a mild-mannered and uncritical animal to make me see in myself those negative attributes that I had always ascribed to *other* American surgeons. Facing two hundred angry men proved to be effective therapy for removing most traces of condescension with which I previously might have regarded them. It also improved my relations with missionary colleagues and with Nepali brothers and sisters in the church. I guess God had no gentler way of removing some of my imperfections; I only wish I could say, for His trouble, that He finished the job. But it was a start.

A Matter of Character

*C*HARACTER-BUILDING experiences lurk around every corner in Nepal. Sometimes innocent objects conspire against us when we're down. Take the mountains of junk in our tiny house, for example. I'm convinced that things sneak around on their own. We no longer ask each other where something is but rather where it's hiding. The inside of our house usually looks like a disaster area in the wake of a tornado, especially when our cook is sweeping, an operation that consists of getting the dirt and dust high in the air and then letting it settle in a different location.

I once used a kerosene pressure lamp to study by early in the morning. If you have never owned such a lamp, you will not appreciate what character-building potential it possesses. At an hour when most sensible people were still asleep, I would spend the first twenty minutes of my day fumbling to get that lamp lit. After that it would begin in earnest to demonstrate its diabolic nature. It would spit, hiss, pop, sputter, fume, blink, smoke, and when I had just about lost my patience, it would suddenly go out, leaving me in total darkness to repeat the sequence. Sometimes it would burst into flames as high as the ceiling, covering everything with fine soot. On the few occasions when I had it going well, it would run out of kerosene or I would jiggle it and the mantel would fall to pieces. In the two months I used it, it gave me second-degree burns of both hands and devoured spare parts like a frog eating fireflies. It was affecting my character so profoundly that I finally had to get rid of the wretched thing and switch to candles.

Among any group of missionaries you can always pick out the Americans. They are the ones loaded with gadgets: still cameras, movie cameras, slide projectors, washing machines, tents, air mattresses, pressure stoves, short-wave radios, binoculars, and you name it. And for those who want to stay one step ahead of the competition . . . well, there's always a piano.

A piano, however, is a source of physical and even spiritual refreshment—unless a string breaks the day before a concert. That happened to Cynthia just before the very first concert she gave for our missionary friends in Amp Pipal. The piano had been badly out of tune, so Cynthia wrote home for some tuning equipment and instructions. The day before the performance Cynthia set to work tuning her piano. She began tightening the first pin with her special tuning hammer, but when she plinked the corresponding note the pitch did not change. So she tightened the pin some more; still no change. She tightened it further; nothing happened. She tightened it once more; finally something happened—the string snapped. It helps to plink the same note you're tightening.

Cynthia collapsed in tears. It would take weeks to get a new string. It could not be mailed because foreigners in Nepal were only allowed two parcels a year, and we'd already gotten our two. Cynthia's only chance of getting a new string for her piano was if someone happened to be coming to Nepal. Since there was nothing else to be done, Cynthia decided to look at the instructions. And there it was: How to fix a broken piano string. Since each end of the string was wound three full turns around its pin and since a string always breaks at one of the

pins, all you had to do, the directions explained, was to
unwind the other pin one and a half turns, advance the wire
along its zigzag course through the inner recesses of the piano
(where it had lain unmolested for the previous fifty years),
pull it up hard, and you would gain exactly one and a half
turns of wire, just enough to wrap around the remaining pin.
What could be simpler?

So guess who got the job. I have trouble fixing familiar
things around the house—what could I do with a piano
string that I knew nothing about? My only help was an Indian
flashlight that blinked on and off like a distress signal at sea,
always going off at a critical moment, as if the ship had sunk
for good—but no, it was on again. And if the light was in a
bad way, you can imagine the state of the sailor in the piano.

Mechanical objects are not the only snares in our path;
living things can lay snares too. Nepal teems with wildlife of
every description—from tiny, curiously shaped and colored
insects to bears, leopards, and even man-eating tigers. The
exploits of some of these creatures are even reported in *The
Rising Nepal*. A recent item told about a tiger that snatched a
nine-year-old girl out of her mother's arms and proceeded to
devour the child right before the mother's eyes. Not far from
Kathmandu, the article said.

Indeed the local fauna contributes much to the exhilaration
of living in Nepal. Getting used to it early is best, because
there is no way to avoid the multitude of living things that
proliferate with abandon on all sides, even inside, of you.
You'll find creatures happily sharing your garden, your
kitchen, your food, your cupboard, your bathroom, and your
bed. You might even say that man's dominion over the animal
kingdom has not yet extended to the hills of Nepal. At least
the animals haven't heard about it.

Probably the most noticeable, certainly the most harmful,

effect of the animal world upon Nepal's human population is caused by those ubiquitous animals no one can see, namely, bacteria and protozoa, which together account for most of the sickness in Nepal. They contaminate drinking water, causing deadly epidemics of dysentery and typhoid fever. They account for the twin scourges of tuberculosis and leprosy, which spread through entire families and neighborhoods, affecting tens of thousands of Nepalis. They take most of the time and energy of the doctors who work here.

In a discussion of Nepal's fauna, bacteria and their associates are really beside the point. After all, one does not adapt to *invisible* objects per se, only to their effects. More to the point are the *visible* creatures, with which we sooner or later must reach an accord if we hope to preserve our sanity.

What would you do, for example, if you found a troop of a thousand ants filing across your dining room floor? You might attack them with brooms, boiling water, stomping feet, or insecticides, but these activities will only cause them to scatter to every corner of your house, ninety percent of them unscathed, and you will be left with a mess to clean. Much better to do nothing at all. In two minutes they will have left, marched off in their columns—except for the few dozen that get waylaid in the sugar bowl. And if you think you can kill ants faster than they can be hatched . . . don't count on it.

Or take flies. We're in favor of certain reasonable measures, like screens, to keep flies out. No matter how many precautions we take, however, some will always manage to get in through holes and cracks around the windows and under the tin roof where the mud and stones don't fill all the gaps. So instead of getting worked up about flies, we remind ourselves to be thankful they only live twenty-four hours. Some clever fellow once calculated that if their lifespan were doubled, within a year the earth would be covered with a layer of flies four inches thick. Having lived in Nepal, I can believe it. We need to count our blessings.

Of the local fauna, the creature you are liable to develop the greatest attachment to is the leech. He proliferates in the rainy season and burrows underground when it turns dry. He waits patiently on leaves and blades of grass for you to pass by, and before you know it, he is onto your shoe, through the lace-hole, into your sock, and sucking your blood. By the time you feel the itch, he is usually gone. The blood oozing into your sock is the only evidence of his visit, except for the itch, which lasts for days if infection doesn't occur, in which case it stops itching and starts hurting.

We used to find it amusing to see how many leech bites a person could get on the twenty-minute walk between the village of Amp Pipal, where some of our colleagues lived, and the hospital. The record was thirty-four, and to my knowledge it hasn't been beaten. On meeting nights during the rains, we would watch each new arrival go through the ritual of pulling off his collection of leeches and then dab pieces of toilet paper onto the bites. Then at some point in the meeting, one or more of the girls present would let out a loud squeal as she spotted a leech woozily stepping end to end across the floor, engorged with a cubic centimeter of someone's blood. The disrupted meeting would not begin again until we all had inspected ourselves and our neighbors for bleeding. Occasionally leeches would bite in unusual locations, which always added to the general interest. The most interesting bites, though, weren't discovered until you got home that night and undressed.

Nepal is widely acclaimed for its abundance and variety of birds. Some are found nowhere else in the world and are gorgeous to behold. However no one mentions the incredible profusion of insects found here, the most beautiful of which are the large and exquisitely painted butterflies. There are hundreds of others, too, that come in a wide assortment of fantastic shapes and hues: some are glistening and iridescent; some have stripes, polka dots, blotches, or borders of brilliant colors; some smell sweet, others stink. Insects are poorly regarded, though. What country ever touted its National Insect? But that need not prevent us from marveling at this part of God's creation. Even the spiders here have gaudy stripes and spots. They also come in the house and take up residence. Some have long hairy legs attached to prune-sized bodies and carry around egg sacs which you had better not burst unless you want two hundred baby spiders running around.

Although I'm constantly being handed the flyswatter by Cynthia and told to eradicate this or that spider that's gotten into her shoe or into the sink or the toilet, I myself am rarely bothered by them. The one exception I can recall was when I discovered a spider the size of a lima bean drowned in my coffee cup. I had just drunk the coffee. It was early in the morning and by candlelight I had mistaken the spider for a lump of undissolved instant coffee. This brings to mind that old story about the three stages of missionary adjustment. First stage: If a fly falls into your coffee cup, you throw out the coffee and get a new cup. Second stage: You pick out the fly and drink the coffee. Third stage: You drink the coffee, fly and all. I haven't heard whether it applies to spiders; maybe that's a fourth stage. If so, I didn't make it.

A small treatise could be written on the fauna of Nepal and its effects on human inhabitants. The reptiles would demand several chapters of their own. Everyone, after all, has a favorite snake story. And I haven't even mentioned the rodent population. Rats, for instance, have been known to chew off the numb fingers of leprosy patients and regularly consume up to twenty percent of a villager's food supply. (The figure is much higher in other parts of the world.) We ourselves are no strangers to the problem, thanks to the community of rats that inhabits our attic. They sponsor nightly sporting events: races, broad jumps, acrobatics. Exploring parties search the kitchen, the pantry, the bathroom. But the worst comes when a rat gets an appendage caught in a trap and bangs about on the plywood ceiling for hours trying to shake loose. It sounds like a late-night replay of the Gunfight at the OK Corral. An alternative to traps is poison, but then the creatures always die in an inaccessible spot, and the house is thick with the smell of rotting rats for days. There are cats, I suppose, but in our experience they have created more problems than they have solved. After twelve years it is fair to say we are no closer to a solution for rats than we were at the start, on which note it is perhaps time to close this brief discussion of Nepal's fauna.

Fortunately missionaries are not called to love the animals of the countries where they work. If that were the case, a lot more missionaries would go home. Yet loving the people isn't always any easier.

A Matter of Adjustment

*H*AVE YOU EVER GOTTEN MAD at a goat for eating your loquat tree? Or at a ring-tailed cat for eating the loquats? Have you ever gotten worked up over having to pay six cents for a five-cent pineapple? Or been rattled by two thousand ants crawling out of your wall just as dinner guests are arriving? Have you ever fired your milkman for adding water to the milk? Or yelled at the gardener for uprooting carrots he thought were weeds? Or been provoked at a porter for asking fifty cents extra for carrying your mother-in-law six miles up a mountain in a basket? If you haven't and think you're missing something, you should come to Nepal.

These examples reveal a great deal about our life here and show how much time and energy can be wasted on matters that are, at best, trivial.

One Christmas we received a letter from a friend back home in which she lamented the bustle and turmoil of life in America and wished she were with us in Amp Pipal. She wanted to celebrate the holidays in peace and quiet, where the simplicity and relaxed pace of life would help her better apprehend the true meaning and spirit of Christmas.

She should have been in our house the day her letter arrived. The cook was being taught for the tenth time how to make pumpkin pudding; the gardener was asking where the broccoli was to be planted; the kerosene refrigerator had stopped working and our month's supply of meat was about to spoil; the banana man, the potato man, and a young teacher soliciting money for a new roof for his school were all at our door; the casserole was burning; the children had just come in covered with mud, but there was no water; and fourteen Nepalis were expected for supper. Don't ever come to our house looking for peace and quiet.

Westerners working in developing countries learn many things about themselves they might never have discovered had they remained at home. The smoothly functioning wheels of Western civilization protect us from many of the grating encounters that are so common abroad and that so acutely test our character and spiritual resources.

Our backgrounds, so oriented to convenience, do little to prepare us for the interminable delays, the unreliable transportation, the limited availability of so-called necessities, and all the other challenges of living in a country like Nepal. So much has been written about "culture shock" and the need to adapt to foreign customs, food, concepts of hygiene, and viewpoints generally that few missionaries get to the field without a thorough indoctrination to the culture of the country to which they are going.

They have learned, in theory at least, that the key to a successful ministry will lie in their ability to assimilate that culture and to free themselves from the attitudes and prejudices of their own. They have been warned about the inevitable feelings of superiority, paternalism, disdain, impatience, and frustration that they are sure to experience and to which they previously may have considered themselves immune. Finally they have been told that the course of their entire missionary career will ultimately depend on one thing: their day-by-day, step-by-step walk with God.

Such preparation is necessary and helpful. In spite of it, I

suspect that most missionaries during their first few years feel
as we did—that they have really botched things up. Intensify-
ing this feeling are friends back home who insist on setting
them on a pedestal and making long excuses for their
mistakes.

One way we found to get whisked off the pedestal was to
have our parents live with us for a couple of months. They
quickly saw that the unpleasant characteristics we had before
we left home had, if anything, become even more apparent.
They must have wondered what the "natives" thought.

Westerners working abroad are continually on display.
Every little thing we do and say is observed, dissected,
discussed, and scattered all over the hills. It is important that
we not lose our cool under such constant scrutiny. But try
keeping your cool with our cook, who can't read, count,
remember, or smell; who can't make the bread come out the
same way two days in a row; who puts cinnamon sugar in the
scrambled eggs and hot peppers in the pancake batter; and
who has at one time or another left out every ingredient of the
pumpkin pudding but the pumpkin. Last time it was the
sugar. Pumpkin pudding can become very important when
you eat it every night, which you have to do when you've
raised two hundred pumpkins and have no place to store
them.

Yet our cook is of inestimable worth. She is honest and
reliable; she loves the children, and her loyalty to us knows no
limit. We stand in awe at the suffering she has endured. She
was married at the age of twelve to an alcoholic who beat her
mercilessly. After three years she ran away and hid in the
woods without food for six days; her aunt finally found her.
She has borne six children and lost five. As a woman in a
Hindu society, essentially without rights, she is compelled to
regard her husband almost as a god and is forbidden even to

pronounce his name, so wide is the gulf between them. She has known nothing but daylong toil and drudgery. She knows, in a way we never will, what it means to be "weary and burdened." For people such as she, Christ's yoke is easy and His burden light. Every time we lose our cool over pumpkin pudding, we feel the millstone around our necks.

You wonder, perhaps, why we have a cook in the first place. In the hills of Nepal, everything is done from scratch—from baking bread to grinding spices—so it takes almost the entire day to prepare meals. There are no frozen or instant foods, no mixes, no meat market. In fact there is no market at all. Vinegar, pickles, mayonnaise, jam—all are made in one fashion or another by our cook. She plucks the chickens, husks the rice, buys the firewood, and cans the vegetables we grow in our garden. If it weren't for our cook, Cynthia would hardly get out of the house and after all, she, too, came to Nepal to treat patients.

One other characteristic of Western culture adds to the difficulty of adjusting to life in Nepal. Most missionaries are so accustomed to life in a mechanized, finely-tuned society, that they are poorly prepared to live among unskilled and largely uneducated people. Limitations like those of our cook are found in varying degrees in many of the Nepalis with whom we work.

For instance for many years I was assisted in the hospital outpatient department by a lovable young chap, whose slowness, inefficiency, and general disorganization tried my patience six times a day, a scenario enhanced by our inability to communicate with each other. Like a little bit of knowledge, a little bit of language often led to more confusion and misunderstanding than if I had never opened my mouth. After I had finished jumping up and down and waving my arms and sending him off in four directions at once, he would smile patiently and sympathetically and say, "Yes sir," which made me feel like a half-inch heel. He was building my character; I wonder what I was doing to his.

Many times a worker arrives in a foreign land only to discover he doesn't love the people quite as much as he thought. They are different; their ways are different. And the new missionary quickly learns that survival depends on his ability to adjust to the new people among whom he plans to live; *he* adjusts to *them,* not vice versa. This is rule number one in any missionary manual.

As is usually the case, however, knowing the rule and following it are two different things. Take something simple, for example, like visitors. Ten times a day, on the average, Nepalis come to our door, singly or in groups. A third of them come to sell; a third come to beg; and a third come to visit or look around. Many are just curious about what goes on inside the houses of these strange white people, and they don't hesitate to stand outside the window looking in.

One of our earliest and most persistent visitors was an unpleasant young fellow who used to come and put his nose up to the living room window and stare inside for minutes on end, trampling all over Cynthia's flowers to get a better view. He was invariably dirty and unkempt, and an insolent leer played incessantly across his stubby-bearded face. Only after several visits did we realize that he was deaf and dumb. "Laato," the local villagers called him. But knowing his condition didn't make his frequent appearances any less annoying. When he wasn't watching through the window, he would sit for hours on our doorstep waiting to be fed. He would grunt and grimace, pointing comically to his supposedly empty stomach. If we fed him, we would have him back every day; if we didn't feed him, he would sit on our stoop until we did. And we weren't the only ones he took advantage

of. Once, after we had given him a large plate of rice, I was
called to the hospital to see a patient. On the way I saw him
eating another large plate of food at the neighbor's. On my
way back from the hospital twenty minutes later, I saw him at
a third house with an even larger plateful, eating more slowly
this time. He gave me a sly grin, happy to let me in on his
little secret. He couldn't have been more pleased with himself.
My feelings weren't so charitable.

Then one day, seeing Laato again with his nose flattened
against the windowpane, I remembered afresh what Jesus had
said about those who feed the hungry and invite in the
stranger and clothe the naked: ". . . whatever you did for one
of the least of these brothers of mine, you did for me"
(Matthew 25:40). I began to see Laato in a new light and no
longer resented his intrusions. His visits occurred less frequently after that, as if, having taught me my lesson, he was
no longer needed.

But it was not a lesson to be learned in a day. Even though
Laato didn't come so often, there were plenty of others to
take his place. As for Laato himself, he had his own reason for
coming less often: We had started making him work for his
meals.

People not only trample the flowers outside our windows;
they pick them, too. In Nepal, picking other people's
flowers—even fruit from their trees—is more or less an
accepted practice: more accepted if you're not caught; less, if
you are. There is even a saying in Nepal that fruit has three
tastes depending on how ripe it is: When green, it has a bitter
taste; when slightly yellow, a sour taste; and when fully ripe,
no taste, because your neighbor has stolen it!

The concept was difficult for us; the flower pickers
especially got to me. They didn't even wait until my back was
turned. I knew I should be happy to let them have all the

flowers they wanted, but it didn't seem fair. They didn't appreciate them much anyway: They'd pick a flower and a moment later toss it away or pull it to pieces. Usually I was able to overlook the loss of a flower or two, or if it looked as if more were about to be picked, I would ask the person please to enjoy the flowers without removing them. But one day a little girl came by to sell firewood—children were the worst offenders—and just as she was leaving, I saw her pluck a particularly large and pretty flower that had just blossomed in one of Cynthia's pots.

Then I did something I had never done before. I went up to her quickly, like a store manager catching a shoplifter, and plucked the flower out of her hand. I got the flower all right. But I also got her dress. I heard a heartsickening rip. The dress was torn all the way down the side; there was nothing underneath.

No matter that I hadn't meant to rip her dress, that I had only meant to give her a little lesson. No matter that the dress was already torn and ragged, barely holding together. At least it had been wearable—probably her only one. She didn't say a word but just looked at me with big eyes while I stood there holding my precious flower.

Our cook came running outside: She never missed anything. Then I saw that an older woman had come with the girl; I recognized her as the mother of my assistant in the outpatient department. Great! The girl suddenly turned and ran down the steps and out the gate. The grandmother followed after her, but not without first giving me a long, inscrutable look, as if she couldn't quite make up her mind just why I had come to their country.

I sent our cook after them, of course, but it was too late to catch the girl: She had run all the way home. But the grandmother came back and accepted my apologies and promised to bring the girl back to our house another day to get some clothes. When we finally said our *namaste's* (the usual Nepali greeting, good for both arrivals and departures), I was still holding the flower. I remember thinking, as I stood there bowing slightly, like *Der Rosenkavelier* with his silver rose, that it's not the situations we encounter in this place that are so unexpected, it's our reaction to them. We don't have to look for entertainment; we make our own.

Whatever else can be said for it, life in Nepal is never dull; it is full of surprises. We are booby-trapped by all sorts of trials and temptations we've never encountered before. The simple fact is that we are far too preoccupied with worldly concerns, varying from the ridiculous to the tragic. Missionaries, of all people, need to free themselves from the distractions that beset them and turn their eyes toward God's eternal purposes.

Aside from the endless minor difficulties that consume so much of our energy, the one aspect of life in Nepal that has presented the greatest challenge to us over the years, has been the whole matter of coping with poverty and its ramifications. How are we to handle the poor and needy when they come hoping for help from the rich missionary?

Some are malingerers, lazy and irresponsible; others have been stricken with misfortune through no fault of their own. It is not easy to tell them apart. Many fall into both categories at once. To give unwisely demeans and creates dependence; to give wisely takes time, which is scarce, and wisdom, which is scarcer. And often the knock comes just as we're going out or sitting down to supper, our third meal. Maybe the knocker hasn't eaten all day and won't find much to eat when he gets home that night. The easiest solution is always the quick handout: It clears our conscience and our doorstep. But we are left with the gnawing thought that the short-range good of such hasty charity will probably be outweighed by its long-range harm.

chapter five

Theorizing about poverty is hard enough, but knowing
what to do when face-to-face with it is much more difficult.
Anyone who has lived in a developing country and has gone
to the beach or out for a picnic has had the experience of
being instantly surrounded by dirty, skinny, runny-nosed,
half-naked children and insolent adolescents, drooling and
grinning at you and rubbing their stomachs, while older folks
stand by to see how you'll react. You do pretty well at first,
smiling and wondering what you can spare from the lunch
basket. Then you try to carry on as if they weren't there. But
more gather to see what the excitement is. They crowd in,
laughing, pointing, spitting. Twenty minutes later you decide
it might be nice if they would move on. You begin to suggest
this by smiling and waving your hand and saying good-by.
But they don't understand, or if they do, they don't let on.
You're the intruder here. But after a while, you begin to think
you have rights too and that they ought to respect them . . .
until you recall that Christians have no rights in this world
and need not expect any.

Finally your kids get fussy and your wife gets cranky. The
day has been spoiled. You try to make the crowd understand
but to no avail. Then, with your expression clouded and your
voice hard, you begin to speak in earnest. Suddenly their faces
change; their mouths fall open; they look surprised and hurt.
A sickening feeling engulfs you—you've done it again. You
remember Christ and His compassion for the multitudes and
try to smile as if you didn't mean it, but it's too late; the
crowd has backed off, sullen and wondering. It's time for you
to go, too. With an empty feeling, you pick up the remains of
your lunch and go to get your coat that you laid aside. It's
gone—stolen. The crowd has gone, too. As you stand there
with a hundred thoughts churning in your mind, you begin
to see once again the truth you've always known: the
compassion of Christ is of God, not man.

An isolated incident? Dramatized? Not in the least. It happens daily, in a hundred different variations, to those who live in the midst of poverty. Even in Nepal, still relatively unspoiled, beggary and theft are increasing because of the rapidly accelerating influx of Western tourists. Living in a poor country, we find ourselves either trusting and pitying people until we get stung, or being on guard and suspicious until we've hurt someone's feelings, with no apparent resting place in between.

As for the crowd around your lunch basket, it is easy to say that if you had known the language, you should have chatted with them, and if you didn't, you should have gotten up and left. But saying that does not take into account the tremendous barrier between their poverty and your wealth. Let them have your whole lunch, and they will begrudge you the basket.

It is hard for friends back home to appreciate just how rich even the poorest missionaries are compared with those around them. Our light is dimmed by the glitter of our goods. We are asked every day for a shirt, money, a tin can, a pair of old shoes, food. If we give to them who ask, we have "rice Christians" and a bigger crowd at our door next day. If we say no, we feel uneasy because we know full well there are seven shirts in the closet we don't really need. The solution for some has been to sell all and live at the level of their neighbors. The rest of us have managed to strike a compromise between that ideal and what we euphemistically call practicality. I am not implying that we are all called to possess nothing, but I am suggesting that if we did, it would help clarify many of Jesus' sayings pertaining not only to poverty but also to discipleship. We can transform everything Jesus said into symbols and metaphors or we can qualify it into thin air; however, in the end the words remain: "Give to the one who asks you, and do

not turn away from the one who wants to borrow from you."
"... sell everything you have and give to the poor, ..."
(Matthew 5:42) "Then come, follow me" (Mark 10:21).

Surely there is a clue here as to how we might remove the barrier between our wealth and their poverty, a barrier that obscures our Christian testimony. Yet in our experience, problems more basic than wealth affect our Christian testimony. Before worrying ourselves over how many shirts to give and how many to keep, we should make sure we are in a place where we can hear what God is saying to us and that we would be willing to "sell everything" if He told us to. If we have really died to self and aren't just kidding ourselves, and if the compassion of Christ is discernible in our lives, then the number of shirts we give and keep is no longer so important, and the barriers created by our wealth largely disappear.

Modern Medicine Comes to the Hills

C OMING TO AN AREA with a half-million people served by only one other missionary doctor and realizing that ninety percent of the people couldn't have cared less whether or not we came was a humbling experience. Most didn't see any advantage in modern medicine; we were simply peddlers selling our wares. Even today many still regard us with lingering distrust and suspicion, unable to comprehend our motive for coming to their land.

The concept of disinterested love is totally foreign to Nepalis because their primary motive for good works is to acquire merit that will benefit them in the next life. Most of our patients have no sense of gratitude for our services; instead, they expect that *we* be grateful to *them* for providing us with an opportunity to gain merit for ourselves. This is why "thank you" is so rarely heard in Nepal; in fact, the Nepali language has no word for it. It's just as well: We wouldn't last long here if we had come to receive thanks.

Skepticism of our work and motives is not the only obstacle blocking the acceptance of modern medicine. Another is ignorance. In rural Nepal, where nearly the entire adult population is unschooled, new ideas do not flourish, and the stubborn adherence to tradition creates an almost insurmountable barrier to change.

Centuries-old customs and superstitions prevent modern

medical and sanitary practices from being accepted. As in all such societies, the nature of most diseases and their means of spreading are largely unknown. Nepalis have a natural reluctance to believe in little germs they cannot see. We doctors are viewed with amusement when we fuss about all sorts of invisible creatures, like bacteria and tiny worms. Even when we point out that the large intestinal worms that *can* be seen are the result of eating little eggs that *can't* be seen, the average adult simply shrugs in disbelief.

Western professionals have implicit faith in the triumph of knowledge over ignorance. All we have to do, we suppose, is *teach* the people, and the scales will fall from their eyes. All very well, in theory. But I remember when one of our most persuasive and fluent community health nurses tried to teach about flies, a relatively simple matter, one would have thought.

Employing that finest product of our Western educational system—the visual aid—she presented to her eager learners a large poster showing a hugely magnified common fly, its great bulbous eyes and long hairy legs graphically displayed in lifelike detail. Wide-eyed with amazement, her listeners gathered around in awed silence as she described the evils of this monstrous insect. She explained how these flies picked up harmful germs and deposited them on food, on plates and glasses, and on sores and cuts. Encouraged by their attentiveness, she described the diseases flies carry, how quickly they reproduce, and how they lay eggs.

When she finished, an animated discussion began among her listeners. It seemed they had been truly impressed by her account of these gigantic British flies (she was from Britain) and were greatly relieved that such creatures were not to be found in Nepal. Did they entertain the notion, too, that she had perhaps come to their country to escape those dreadful flies? Ah teacher, teach thyself.

The manner of life in rural Nepal does nothing to protect unsuspecting Nepalis from the hordes of pathogenic bacteria that constantly surround them. Nepalis prepare and serve their meals on mud floors. The mud, called *lipnu* is a mixture of red clay and buffalo dung, applied fresh each day. They eat with their fingers, ceremonially rinsing them before the meal with water from a brass pot. The amount of water they use is hardly enough to get rid of the gross dirt, let alone the germs. Water is used sparingly in Nepal, because it must be carried in an earthenware crock from a spring that is often half an hour away. Even if they believed in using soap, they couldn't afford it at the price of half a day's wages; besides, it would make the food taste bad.

Water in Nepal is not only scarce, it is often contaminated. And if the water is not, the receptacles are. But Nepalis resist boiling their water because it flattens the taste and uses up their already limited supply of firewood. The worst contaminant of all, of course, is human feces, which is widely distributed. Latrines and outhouses are a curiosity, and the progressive citizen who ventures to construct such a facility usually abandons the whole project after a week because the place stinks so badly. Aside from the effluvium, which can be controlled with a little lime, another major deterrent to the acceptance of outhouses is the widespread belief that the spirits will get you if you use the same place twice. A few high-caste Nepalis cover their stool, carrying with them a little spade for that purpose, but this practice has mostly died out. At a recent public meeting, however, I heard a young Nepali schoolteacher attempt to resurrect the custom. He concluded his speech by telling his listeners that they had less sense than cats: Cats at least knew to cover their droppings.

Ignorance concerning nutrition is another major obstacle to improving Nepal's standard of health. The land produces too little food as it is, so Nepalis cannot afford to misuse what they have. Ignorance of nutrition leads to poor nutrition. Poor nutrition leads to lessened resistance, then to debilitating illness, which leads to decreased farm productivity because farmers are too weak to work, which leads again to poor crops, which causes worse nutrition—a wrong-way cycle perpetuated by habit and superstition.

Nowhere are the effects of poor diet and decreased resistance so devastating as in children—many of whom die of malnutrition. And as if Nepalis don't have enough trouble fighting off sickness, their problems are aggravated instead of alleviated by such pernicious and long-entrenched notions as the advisability of withholding food from the sick (in particular, fluid from dysentery patients) and a host of lesser prohibitions, such as not feeding bananas to people with colds or pumpkins and cucumbers to postpartum women.

In addition there are numerous, purely religious food restrictions that are detrimental to health. One of these, for example, prohibits Brahmins from eating eggs, thus depriving their children, especially, of an important source of protein.

Untroubled by modern medical knowledge, average Nepalis have no reason to be concerned about nutrition, stool disposal, water contamination, or general cleanliness. They believe the diseases they contract are the work of spirits or witches. And in the case of conditions that affect the nervous system, such as meningitis, tetanus, and epilepsy, this notion is more plausible than our scientific explanations. Consequently Nepalis resort to the services of priests and shamans (witch doctors) to placate or exorcise these evil forces and engage in costly rituals to insure recovery. Only the more enlightened seek our medical services when symptoms appear, and then only for certain types of ailments.

Although acceptance of modern medicine is increasing,

greater reliance is still placed on the advice and therapy of village "practitioners" than on the treatment we provide. And priests have the last word on any matter as important as health. Not all the nostrums of the local "doctors" are harmful; both priests and shamans seem to benefit many of their patients. In addition, they fulfill an important socio-psychotherapeutic function in the community; they some-times make people better when we do not. I once told a nervous young man with impotence that there was no medicine for his condition. He said he'd gotten some before from a village doctor that had worked wonders for two years. So I sent him off to get some more of the same; I wish I knew what it was.

On the other hand, many patients arrive at our hospital nearly dead, having been treated for days or weeks in their homes with various herbs and lotions, some of them danger-ous poisons. And when we fail to revive them, doubt concerning the effectiveness of our medicine increases. Even after patients are inside the hospital, our efforts are thwarted by certain fiercely held family beliefs. For instance, well-meaning relatives will pour water down the throat of an unconscious patient to prevent his spirit from getting thirsty and leaving the body prematurely. The water runs into his lungs and chokes him, usually resulting in his death; and presto, one more failure is chalked up to modern medicine.

Most distressing of all, however, is the custom of taking very sick patients out of the hospital so they can die near a river, thereby securing the rapid and unimpeded transport of their souls into the next life. We have worked over many patients for hours and days, only to have the family take the person away to the river just at the critical point when we expected recovery to begin. After years of battling with relatives, we finally learned why they were so adamant: they believe that unless the patient's spirit passes into the water before death, it will escape from the body and wander about to haunt living family members. Thus it is not so much concern for the patient but concern for themselves that prompts the relatives' vehemence.

There is a final way in which Nepalis suffer because of their religious traditions and beliefs. Many priests and shamans in rural areas extort money and goods from people who come to them for help in times of illness, crop failure, and other natural catastrophes. For example, a destitute, elderly man with jaundice, who had once been a well-to-do and influential member of his community, came to our hospital. He had spent his entire life savings and sold all his possessions, and those of his family, to be cured by a priest. All he had was a gallstone. His is a common story; it is no wonder that so many of our patients cannot pay their hospital bills, or worse yet, cannot afford to come to the hospital at all.

Among the poor, the greatest single deterrent to the acceptance of modern medicine is not ignorance or religious beliefs, but lack of money. As proof of this, before we began to offer free cataract operations, we had virtually no patients; now that the operation is subsidized by a charitable organization, it is the most common procedure we do—about a hundred a year. (The operations are subsidized by Operation Eyesight Universal in Calgary, Alberta.)

Poverty is a relative concept. If a Nepali could rise anywhere near to what Americans consider the poverty level, he would be the richest man in his district. Living in America costs more, we say, and indeed, that accounts for some of the discrepancy. But the cost of living in America is high mainly because of the high *standard* of living we have set for ourselves, below which, we feel, life would be intolerable. But what is intolerable for us in the West would be inconceivable luxury to a village Nepali.

Most rural Nepalis possess only the very minimum necessary to survive: a small house of mud and stone, a few goats and chickens, a wooden plow, a couple of pots, plates, and other implements, one or two blankets per family, some straw mats, and often only one set of clothes per person. The thirty percent or so that make up the "middle class" might own a cow or some buffalos and enough land to produce food for a whole year. They will have an extra set of clothes, an umbrella, dark glasses, and maybe even a pair of shoes. And if they are upper middle class, they will own a transistor radio, the supreme status symbol. The one percent that are still richer are usually absentee landowners who long ago moved to Kathmandu. They alone would be above our American poverty line.

Very few Nepalis living in the hills have a regular income; paying jobs are few and far between. The few that do are usually the poorest because they are the ones with no land of their own. They live from hand to mouth by doing menial work, such as carrying loads. Nepal's per capita annual income is about one hundred and forty dollars, but the average income of Nepalis living in our area would be only a fraction of that amount. Even most of the Nepalis who do own land cannot fully support themselves from it. So for parts of the year, they must buy food—with what little money they have—or get by on one meal a day. As a result medical treatment is a luxury they cannot usually afford.

Obviously patients are going to wait to see if they are really sick before deciding to go to the hospital. Nepalis are understandably hesitant about traveling to a strange place to accept treatment at the hands of even stranger white-faced foreigners. Furthermore a journey to the hospital seriously disrupts the necessary routines of farm and family life. Nepalis rarely travel alone, so usually patients are accompanied by

family members and by friends as well. Patients often arrive
with a contingent of eight or ten persons, many of whom
want an examination themselves since they have come so far.

Making arrangements for a trip to the hospital is no easy
matter. Reliable neighbors must be found to tend to the
children and animals left behind; men to carry the patient
must be hired; food for the party must be carried from home
or purchased in Amp Pipal at inflated prices. In the end the
hospital bill sometimes wipes away many months of savings.
It is no wonder then that of all the people in the area we serve,
probably no more than half would even consider it feasible to
come to the hospital, even if they wanted to. Neither is it
surprising that many of those who finally do come arrive too
late.

Someone has to pay the bill for medical care, even if the
patient cannot. The government offers free treatment at its
facilities; but although there's no charge, there's often no
medicine either. The government's health budget amounts to
only thirty cents per head, and that does not go far, even in
Nepal. Mission hospitals, on the other hand, must charge fees
to keep operating, although those same fees discourage many
people from coming. For example, a Nepali is going to think
twice before spending two days' wages on an X-ray or two
months' wages on an operation. For those without any
income, treatment at the mission hospital, except for a few of
our cheapest pills, is out of the question.

This is the terrible dilemma that confronts almost every
missionary doctor in the world: How to meet the needs of the
poor and at the same time keep the hospital running. If
anyone has found a solution, this doctor would be grateful to
hear it.

In addition to ignorance and poverty, our patients have
other obstacles to overcome. One is the simple matter of

logistics. There are no roads. Patients too sick to walk are carried on men's backs. Most patients journey a whole day to get to our hospital. (A day's walk for a Nepali would take two days for the average American, who might need admission just to recover from the trip.)

The hospital's location near the top of a mountain does not make things any easier; however, neither does it add to the overall difficulty. The population in the hills is distributed evenly, with about the same number of people living on the mountains as in the valleys; so there would be the same climb, coming or going, no matter where the hospital was.

Seasonal factors also limit a villager's access to medical care. During certain periods of the year, most patients simply cannot come to the hospital. Rice planting and rice harvesting seasons, for example, require the presence of every member of the family lest the entire year's crop be jeopardized. At such times no one can be spared to accompany the sick person to the hospital; the survival of one individual must be subordinated to the welfare of the whole family.

Neither do patients come for treatment during the frequent religious festivals; what's more, those already in the hospital abruptly leave because of their desire to be at home during the holidays.

Finally, the monsoon rains prevent many families from traveling to the hospital. The swollen rivers, so easily forded in the dry season, can be crossed only on one of the few all-weather bridges, which may be a one-to-two-day walk out of the way. Many can't even get to a bridge; they are completely isolated.

It is fortunate for us, however, that so many do not come: If they did, we would be hopelessly swamped with work. As it is, we have watched the people come in greater and greater numbers over the years; now we have reached the point where we can take no more.

Yet the unmet needs remain enormous. The greatest part of the suffering we don't even see, not only because so many do not come but because most of those who do come have already endured most of their suffering at home. Minor illnesses often become major ones because patients delay going to the hospital. A toothache, for instance, is surely a minor problem. But if *you* had to walk a whole day or more to get to your dentist, you might procrastinate, too, hoping it would go away—until your jaw became infected, your face so swollen that you couldn't see, and your throat so swollen that you couldn't swallow. The examples are legion.

Suffering has many faces, and sooner or later, it affects nearly everyone. But the sad part is that most of it is unnecessary. Half the population, for instance, is infested with worms, yet it takes only ten cents worth of medicine to cure a person—if there were someone to give it. Children are crippled for life simply because some minor burn or fracture went untreated. Worst of all, half the children born in rural Nepal die before they reach the age of five, usually in their first year, and almost entirely of illnesses that are easily treatable. As a result of this high infant mortality rate, the average life expectancy in Nepal is one of the lowest anywhere in the world. (The current nationwide figure is forty-four, but in the hills it is closer to thirty-five.) If only our minds could translate these cold statistics into human terms, we might begin to grasp the enormity of the suffering that's so much a part of every Nepali family.

The half-million people served by the Amp Pipal Hospital are distributed over an area the size of Rhode Island. When the hospital was being built in the late 1960s, there were no other functioning medical facilities in the entire region, except a small dispensary run by the missionaries in Amp Pipal itself. The hospital started in 1970 with one Canadian doctor, Dr.

Helen Huston, and has since added three more. Four doctors is still far from the five hundred doctors available for every half-million Americans.

In recent years a government doctor has been assigned to a newly built district hospital six hours' walk away, but long periods go by when he is somewhere else. The government has great difficulty staffing its rural hospitals, since doctors here, as everywhere, prefer lucrative jobs in the cities. The government, however, has taken steps to expand its medical services, and one step has been the opening of a medical school in Kathmandu. Formerly Nepalis had to study outside the country to become doctors, and very few openings were available. Still it will be many years before the people in the hills have anything near the number of doctors they need. A second step of even greater importance is the numerous health posts created throughout Nepal that are staffed by government-trained paramedical workers. This program promises to bring basic medical care within the reach of almost every village. But this promise, too, will take years to realize. In the meantime most of the people in the area we serve will remain without effective, affordable medical service.

When the Amp Pipal hospital was constructed, there were no roads in the entire region. Building materials had to be brought in by airplane to the landing strip six miles away or over the four-to-five-day foot trail from Kathmandu. Aside from the interesting logistics involved in constructing a hospital under such conditions—and near the top of a mountain as well—the local builders who were hired had never seen a hospital before, much less built one. Nevertheless, as a result of the vision and resolution of Dr. Huston and the hard work of the other missionaries with her, the Amp Pipal Hospital became a reality. Those visiting Amp Pipal for the first time are always surprised to discover a hospital set out among such remote and wild hills. In one sense, it is an anomaly; in a deeper sense, it is a remarkable instance of God's provision for these people.

The building itself can accommodate up to forty inpatients. There are two operating rooms, an X-ray unit, and rudimentary laboratory facilities. The pharmacy stocks the basic drugs we need, and in spite of the chronic difficulty in procuring supplies, the hospital is sufficiently equipped to handle most medical problems that arise.

The number of patients treated at the hospital has risen dramatically over the years. Between 35,000 and 40,000 outpatients are seen each year. In the past six years the total volume of surgery has tripled, and major surgical cases alone have increased fivefold. Over 1,200 surgical procedures are performed each year. Both the hospital and its staff have been stretched to the limit.

The financial policy of the United Mission to Nepal requires that, insofar as possible, each of its hospitals be self-supporting, except for foreign medical staff, who are supported from abroad. Outside grants are also given for the treatment of such diseases as tuberculosis and leprosy and for the care of the poor generally. Fees received from patients cover most of the hospital's running costs, including the salaries of its sixty Nepali employees. The fees, by any standard, are extremely low. The average cost of an outpatient visit is $1.30; the average inpatient day, including all treatment, comes to $2.50. The daily bed fee is twenty-five cents. A major operation costs $12.00. Still, for the village Nepali, these prices hurt.

Mission institutions, as a rule, cannot expect to be permanently supported from outside sources. Individuals and agencies back home are much more inclined to give money for new and exciting projects, rather than to maintain old ones. Furthermore, anticipating that the various institutions established by the United Mission will eventually be nationalized, to leave behind schools and hospitals the government will be unable to finance once the mission withdraws would be a disservice to Nepal.

These realities require us to be firm in the collection of fees, an aspect of our work that is naturally unpleasant. Curing a patient's illness is one thing; demanding his next three months' wages to pay for it is another. Fortunately we have compassionate and discerning Nepali cashiers who spare the medical staff this task. In addition most of our patients are able and willing to pay at least part of their bills. For those who can't pay in full, the fee is adjusted according to their circumstances, and we never refuse medical care simply because a patient cannot pay. Up to twenty-five percent of our overall service is given free of charge, the loss to the hospital being made up by outside funds and to a lesser extent by the paying patients, whose rates are fixed at a level to accommodate some degree of charity work.

When the hospital opened, very few trained Nepali staff were available, so classes to train assistant nurses were begun. Such training still remains an important part of the hospital program. Most of the staff learned their jobs in Amp Pipal, although in recent years as national training programs have gotten under way, we have recruited government-trained workers as well. A Nepali nurse has been trained to take over the post of nursing superintendent, and our ultimate goal is to turn the entire operation of the hospital over to qualified and suitable Nepali doctors. So far, however, none have been found who are willing to live in Amp Pipal.

How does a forty-bed hospital provide reasonable medical care for such a large population? Obviously it doesn't begin to, mainly because so few are able to make the long trip. For those who do come, we attempt to provide medical care comparable to what is available in the average small American hospital. Because our personnel and facilities are limited, we must concentrate our efforts on those patients who stand a reasonable chance of receiving benefit from our treatment. It is painful to have to send away those who in larger medical centers might be helped, but to whom we have little to offer. Often patients with incurable illnesses, who have been carried for two or three days to reach the hospital, arrive hoping to be cured by an injection or an operation. Happily, though, for the great majority who come there is much we can do.

Krishna

*T*HE SMALL SPINDLY BOY sitting in my office complaining of burning urine didn't make much of an impression on me. He was one of eighty or ninety patients that day. After a cursory exam, I sent him away with a little medicine and less thought and turned to the next patient. I had not noticed who brought him, which wasn't surprising since no one had. For an adult to come unaccompanied is unusual; for a child to come alone is virtually unheard of.

A week later he was back, unaffected by my therapy. Again he had come alone, a two-hour walk from where he lived. When I asked why no one from his family had brought him, he said he had no family.

His name was Krishna, and although he was nine, he was about the size of an average American five-year-old. His father had died in a landslide years before, and his mother had moved away to live with another man and left Krishna in the haphazard care of some neighbors. I took a greater interest in him this time—not only because my treatment had failed, but also because of the winsome way he asked me for some better medicine. His manner was characterized by a conflicting mixture of helplessness and a certain worldly wisdom born, I supposed, from fending for himself.

Krishna's urine was badly infected, so I sent him off again with some stronger medicine. But a week later he was back with his condition unchanged. An X-ray revealed a stone the size of a baseball in his bladder, which explained why his urine was infected and why our medicine had not worked.

We contacted the family with whom Krishna had been living, and they consented to surgery as long as it was free. A problem arose, however, over who would stay in the hospital with him. We met with a representative of the panchayat, who, after some coaxing, eventually agreed to arrange for various people from the neighborhood to take turns caring for Krishna during the postoperative period.

"Everyone is planting corn just now," he explained to me. "No one has spare time to sit in the hospital. But I'll do the best I can."

On the stipulated day, the panchayat representative himself brought Krishna to the hospital, and the next morning I removed his bladder stone. I performed the operation under spinal anesthesia, and although Krishna remained wide-awake throughout the procedure, he showed neither fear nor apprehension. In some ways, the boy seemed mature and hardened far beyond his years.

During the early postoperative period, Krishna's condition progressed satisfactorily. A few days following surgery, I gave Krishna his bladder stone to keep as a souvenir. (I generally return to its owner each stone I remove; it not only provides proof that my diagnosis was correct, but it also serves to convince skeptical villagers of the efficacy of surgery.) As I handed Krishna his stone, he said not a word but carefully, almost reverently, held it in both of his hands, as if it were the most precious gem in the world. Watching him, I suddenly realized that the stone I had so casually given him was the only object he had ever handled that he could call his own. Even the tattered clothes on his back were the castoffs of other children. The stone remained under his pillow for the next week until a dense fellow from Krishna's village dropped it on the cement floor to see if it would break. It did, and Krishna's heart with it. I never saw the stone again.

When Krishna did not recover as quickly as expected, the villagers began to lose interest and gradually stopped coming to bring him food. Even the old man who had been most regular and faithful announced he could stay no longer.

"You can take care of him from now on," he told me. "Do it for your religion's sake."

Before I could think of a way around that, he was gone.

A combination of malnutrition and urinary-tract infection led to a steady deterioration in Krishna's condition. He became listless and stopped eating in spite of our attempts to provide him with tasty food. He seemed to be caught in that irreversible sequence of events that leads inexorably to death from starvation and that we had seen so many times before. For days he lingered, long after we had given up hope. Then, imperceptibly at first and for no detectable reason, his condition slowly began to improve. During the long vigil, not one person from his village came to see him.

We decided to keep Krishna in the hospital until he was strong enough to survive the marginal diet he could expect to get in his village. Krishna's survival was important not only for his own sake, but for the sake of others as well. If he were to succumb after leaving the hospital, the operation would be blamed, and many others needing simple operations would decline to undergo such fearful treatment.

As Krishna neared recovery, I would say to him each day when I made rounds, "Soon you'll be ready to go home."

Each day he would look up with pleading eyes and answer, "Please don't send me away from here."

I thought to myself, *He's gotten to like our food too much.* I did send him home. Most Nepali orphans are absorbed into the life of the community quite satisfactorily, even if they have no proper relatives to care for them. Krishna had spent most of his life in the village; clearly that was the place for him to stay.

The next time I saw Krishna, he was almost dead. Our plan had not worked. Three weeks in the village without adequate food and attention had reduced him to a skeleton. He was too weak to even raise his head.

The same old man brought him in. "He's yours now," he said. "We can't do anything for him."

I found out from the old man that there had been considerable discussion among the villagers as to the nature of Krishna's malady. Some believed the spirit of a witch had entered the wound during the surgery and was continuing to exert its power over the boy. Belief in witches was widespread in our area of Nepal, and the village shamans, whose function was to neutralize the power of witches, never lacked for business. The witches themselves were people actually living in the neighborhood who were alternately shunned and placated by the other villagers. Since their office was usually hereditary, most were aware of their designation and consciously used their power to intimidate anyone who crossed them.

But witches had little power over healthy persons; they exerted their influence only on those rendered vulnerable by an ordinary illness or a wound through which the witch could enter its victim directly. The latter was thought to have happened in Krishna's case; a very powerful witch had been implicated, and consequently, many of the villagers had dismissed Krishna as hopeless. At the same time, many villagers were awed that I was able to remove a big stone from a little boy's belly. Just maybe, I'd have another trick up my sleeve; they would give me one more chance.

I almost wished they had spared me the trouble. As I looked at the emaciated and nearly lifeless figure stretched on the examining table before me, I was inclined to cast my vote with those who had given up hope. Krishna's basic problem was starvation, compounded by persistent infection. Since there was little likelihood that he could eat on his own, we fed him by tube for the first several days. To our relief and surprise, he responded rapidly and within a week was alert, bright-eyed, and eating with increasing appetite. A little food can do wonders for a person; our medicine played no more than a secondary role, if that. We went through our limited selection of antibiotics one by one, but none had any appreciable effect on Krishna's infection.

After a month Krishna had regained most of his weight and strength and was well on his way to becoming a fixture at our hospital. The healthier he became, the greater a problem he posed for us: With his incurable infection, he would not survive for long in his village; yet how could he be kept indefinitely at the hospital? The longer he stayed, the more difficult it would be to send him home.

From time to time as I made my rounds, I would remind him that he would have to return to his village when he was well enough. Invariably he would become downcast and beg for more time, for work, for anything to avoid leaving the hospital. Whenever I felt myself softening, I would remind myself of all the reasons it was not right for him to stay: The hospital was not a good environment; it wasn't natural; we couldn't feed him forever; the village had a responsibility to fulfill. What would happen when we foreigners had to leave? What would happen when the government took over the hospital? It was important to resist these unrealistic, but heartfelt, feelings, which moved us to keep Krishna with us instead of sending him back to his village.

Resist them I did. Finally the day came, after three months in the hospital, when Krishna was to be discharged. I had already attempted to contact the people of his village but had received no response. No one would come to get him; they had washed their hands of him. So I determined to send him alone. He had come and gone alone when he first came to us; he could go alone again. It was only a two-hour walk.

Krishna did not believe me when I told him that *now* was the time to go.

"How can I go when it's about to rain?" he protested.

I looked outside and said I thought the rain would hold off until he reached home, especially as the sun was shining brightly.

"The sun will burn me, then," he said.

I remarked that some large clouds were about to cover the sun, which would make it ideal for walking. It occurred to me that this little boy was a real con artist, playing on my sympathy for all it was worth. I even entertained the notion that the villagers had been putting him up to it to get him out of their hair. I was forgetting, of course, that not a soul had been to see him for three months.

When I turned to leave him, he gave me one last uncomprehending look, as if he couldn't believe that what he had found at our hospital was illusory after all. For my part, I reflected that sometimes one had to make hard decisions in this business. Conveniently I had no doubt as to the right decision: In the long run, it was in Krishna's best interest that he return to his village—that was that.

Krishna didn't see it that way. On a Saturday afternoon two weeks after I had sent him home, he came back again, this time to our house. He was a little thinner than when he had left the hospital.

"What have you come for?" I asked by way of greeting.

"I want to stay here and work for you," he said.

"What's wrong with staying in your village?"

"They don't want me there. They don't feed me. Instead, they beat me."

"Now, Krishna, don't tell me that in Nepal they beat children. People here love children."

"They love their own children," he answered sullenly. "But they don't love me."

"Well," I said, coming directly to the point, "it's completely out of the question for you to stay here. We have no way to take care of you, no place for you to live, no work for you to do. You must go back to your village." I spoke kindly, but firmly.

"How can I go back there? I'm sick. I've come for medicine."

"You shouldn't have come on a Saturday, then," I told him. "You knew the hospital would be closed. You can't get medicine today."

"Then let me sleep in the hospital tonight; I'll get medicine tomorrow," he pleaded.

I thought he was being a bit of a rascal. I could appreciate why the villagers might be happy to be rid of him. Reasoning that to give in would be merely putting off today's problem until tomorrow, I said, "No. You go home now, and come back for your medicine another day."

Then, looking me straight in the eye, he said, "Don't make me go back there. I have no home. I am a child without a father. You are my father. You are the only father I have." He said it without calculation, as if, indeed, that were the fact of the matter.

Something inside me was saying, *Watch out. You're being taken*. I knew there were children in every country who learned at an early age to strike chords of sympathy in unwary adults as their only means of survival. Surely this little boy before me was a master at this art. He had struck a resounding chord.

We had been sitting on the front steps, side by side. We remained there for a long time in silence while I mulled over all the reasons why it was my duty to send him back to his village, regardless of whether he had been putting on an act for my benefit. The reasons were numerous, obvious, and compelling. To spare Krishna and myself the emotional trauma of the moment by acceding to his request would be to invite the certain and much more severe problems of separation and adjustment in the future, not to mention the question of who would look after Krishna in the meantime. I thought of the precedent it would set. We would be deluged with orphans the minute the word got out. Up until now we had been very careful not to get involved taking in unwanted children. Wasn't it enough to have come to this place, to care for the sick until they recovered, to feed them if they were hungry, and to pay their bills if they had no money? Did our Christian duty demand adopting them as well?

"Krishna, you must go home. Now."

He burst into tears.

My decision had been right, but I was wrong. Krishna cried for a long time. Along with his tears, he poured out his heart to me—his fears, his loneliness, his longing for a home and for affection. My mind went back to an evening some weeks earlier when I had haltingly tried to explain the meaning of James 1:27 to our Nepali Bible class: "Religion that God our Father accepts as pure and faultless is this: to look after orphans and widows in their distress and to keep oneself from being polluted by the world." That passage, I learned, is the only place in the New Testament where the word "orphan" is used. The verse had not impressed me then; in fact, I had been unable to figure out why James defined "pure and faultless" in such odd terms. As I sat there listening to Krishna, however, the verse began to take on a new meaning for me. It meant that if I were not ready to care for orphans in their distress, then there was something very wrong with my religion. Not being content with my exegesis of His verse, God seemed further to be asking me, "If you are not ready to care for *this* orphan in his distress, who are you ever going to care for?"

That day, Krishna did not return to his village. Instead, he stayed at the hospital while we sought God's leading. We finally arranged for him to live in a Christian orphanage in Kathmandu, where he made many friends and eventually professed faith in Christ.

The Doctor Knows Best

D OCTORS ARE SUPPOSED to save lives; but occasionally the opposite is the case. Doctors can do people harm. They even do people in.

Among doctors, surgeons fail most dramatically. Failure comes in many forms and for many reasons, often as a result of error, although sometimes it just seems to happen without known cause. Especially unlucky is the patient who suffers the surgeon's failure twice.

One chilly February afternoon, a young couple brought their eight-month-old infant to us. The night before, the sleeping child had rolled into the fireplace and had badly burned both feet. As is common in Nepali homes, the fireplace was merely a depression in the middle of the living room floor with no barricade around it. The family was poor and had inadequate clothing for the cold winter nights, so they huddled close to the embers for warmth—too close. This was their first child.

The father, about twenty, had an open and trusting expression. His wife was a slight teenage girl to whom the hospital was an incomprehensible and frightening place. They were simple villagers, living in a tiny one-room, stone-and-mud house only a two-hour walk from the hospital. They owned a small plot of land on which they were able to grow enough food to feed themselves for about three months of the year; for the remainder, they worked in other men's fields and did odd jobs.

Burns are one of the conditions we most dread treating. Small and superficial burns present no problem; they hardly need treatment. But the deeper ones invariably require a long hospital stay, innumerable dressings, skin grafting, and then more dressings. Nepalis generally are not prepared to accept a long hospitalization or, if they seem agreeable at the outset, they often become impatient and change their minds after the treatment has begun.

This baby's burns involved mainly his feet. The toes and soles in particular were badly charred. If the child were ever to be able to walk, the burned areas would need skin grafts. The wounds would not be ready for grafting for three weeks, and complete healing would take two more weeks. I explained to the young parents what had to be done. After much discussion and persuasion, they finally agreed to have the child admitted to the hospital for treatment. The greatest problem arose when the mother refused to remain alone in the hospital with the child: She insisted her husband stay, too, even though it meant giving up his work, upon which the family's livelihood depended. She could not get over her fear of the strange foreign doctors and nurses, the dismal prisonlike concrete floors and walls, the periodic screams emanating from the children's ward, and the other unpleasant and alarming sights, sounds, and smells of a busy and overcrowded mission hospital. I brushed aside the husband's worry about how he was going to feed his family by blandly assuring him that nothing mattered as much as whether his son would be able to walk. Supposing I must know best, he agreed to stay.

All went according to schedule, and about three weeks later the burn wounds were ready to be grafted. During this period the parents had decided several times to take their baby home and were only dissuaded by the concerted efforts of the hospital staff—together with the relatives of other patients, who seldom missed the chance to piously rebuke *anyone else* for not following the doctor's orders.

The grafting was performed uneventfully, but after about four days, the graft on one foot became infected and much of it dissolved away, especially on the sole of the foot where it was most needed. There was nothing to do but repeat the grafting on that foot, lest all the trouble and time already invested should come to nothing.

But the child's parents didn't see it that way. They had reached their limit. This latest development gave them reason to doubt my word. Confident that I knew better than they what should be done and that they would agree if I were only forceful enough, I proceeded by every means I knew to persuade them to accept the repeat grafting. Without getting a definite response from them, but convinced they would see it my way in the end, I went ahead and scheduled the regrafting. But when the time came to call for the child to be brought to the operating room, the parents adamantly refused. So I went to the children's ward myself. With the omniscient air of a surgeon, I gently but firmly said to the parents, "We *must* do this, you know. Don't be stubborn. Think of your child's entire future life; you mustn't wreck it." Then I took the child from the arms of the unresisting mother, paused for a moment, and walked slowly away to the operating room. No one had moved; not another word had been spoken.

We used ether, the same anesthetic we had used for the first skin grafting, to put the child to sleep. The graft was taken from the thigh with an electric dermatome and laid in place on the raw surface of the foot. I took great care in applying the dressing, lest I dislodge the newly placed pieces of skin. As I was wrapping on the last outer layer of the dressing, I suddenly noticed that the baby had stopped breathing. I grabbed a stethoscope and listened; no beat at all. One of the most dreaded complications of any operation had occurred: cardiac arrest.

Forgetting the skin graft I had just painstakingly dressed, I began to pump the heart by pushing up and down on the anterior wall of the chest. The child's pupils were fixed and dilated. Every few minutes I listened anxiously for the return of the heartbeat—nothing. I put a small tube down the trachea so we could use a respirator bag to breathe for the baby. Five minutes passed—no heartbeat. I continued pumping and praying. Ten minutes—no beat. Fifteen minutes—I had given up hope. Twenty minutes—what was I going to say to the parents now? Twenty-five minutes—*this is absurd. No one ever comes back this long after a cardiac arrest. I'll pump five more minutes and then quit.*

After the last five minutes, I absently listened to the heart a final time. Nothing . . . or was there? It couldn't be. I was hearing my own heart pumping. But no, there *was* something there. The child's heart was beating! And then as I watched, the child took a short gasp of breath, and another, and another. At first the breathing was jerky and uneven, but soon it became regular. I could hardly believe the child was going to make it. God seemed to be playing games with me by plunging me into a pit of despair only to lift me out by performing a miracle at the last minute. There was no sensible explanation. But the trauma of the episode numbed any sense of relief and gratitude I ordinarily would have felt. And a gnawing uncertainty remained: Was the baby really okay? When it came time to return the child to the children's ward, I was still deeply worried about his condition. The parents suspected nothing.

My worries were justified. An hour later the child still slept. Another hour went by. Three hours. Four. Still no sign of consciousness.

The father said, "Last time he didn't take this long to wake up. Is anything wrong?"

"Sometimes it takes a little longer than usual," I responded. Knowing when to reveal the whole truth so as not to arouse unnecessary alarm is never easy. When I came back after supper, the only signs of life were the wheezy respirations and the beating heart. But a new symptom had appeared: a funny twitching of the mouth, which was not a good sign. The baby was having a convulsion. I could no longer delay; I told the parents the child had suffered a serious complication from the anesthesia and that his brain had been damaged. I couldn't say if he would recover.

The couple took the news with little show of emotion. I searched their faces, trying to see what they were thinking. I saw nothing except that deep sorrow so common among the very poor when they are given one further crushing burden to carry. No bitterness or anger; not even a sense of betrayal. Just uncomprehending sorrow.

Day after day went by and the baby did not wake up. Two to three times a day I faced the parents, and each day brought less hope. The convulsions stopped. The skin graft took; the feet healed beautifully. But the patient did not awake.

After a month the father said to me simply, "We have no more hope. We must go. Already our corn crop has been lost. If I cannot get work quickly, we will have no food at all."

The mother wept as they left the hospital. She knew she would be unable to keep her baby alive once they got home. She had believed until then that somehow I would make her baby able to walk, as I had said. I watched them go and wondered anew why God so often chose to teach me at the expense of others—especially such as these.

Four months later the father came to see me. The baby had died shortly after they arrived home. As for himself, someone else had taken his job while he had been staying in the hospital with his baby. He was looking for work and hoped I could give him a job. He had given his small plot of land to a wealthy man in his village as security against an urgently needed loan; he would probably never get his land back. He had no money, no land, no job. His wife was pregnant. Could I help?

I had heard this story many times: A man without work desperately forfeits his land to get money to eat, and when his money is gone, he shows up at our door begging for a job. But this time the story had a significant difference; this time I had been part of the problem.

I had no job to give him. And even if a job had been open, dozens had asked ahead of him. Besides, we could hardly be expected to provide jobs to compensate for each surgical failure, or so the nursing superintendent told me when I inquired.

Somehow the family managed to keep going. The new baby was born, and then another. The father got an occasional odd job hauling stones in a basket for our builder. This provided just enough money to keep food in their stomachs. And every month he came by to ask if a permanent job at the hospital had become available.

His chance finally came. One of the sweepers was retiring, and the nursing superintendent, finally relenting, decided to give the father the vacant job. Three years had passed since he had brought his child to the hospital, and now as I daily watched him cheerfully and contentedly working, my painful memories began to fade. I occasionally saw his wife with her two bouncing children; her sorrows seemed to have faded, too. It was a happier ending than any of us would have dared believe possible.

chapter eight

I had only one misgiving. I wondered whether the father, now that he was working in the hospital, would use his position to try and dissuade other patients from undergoing surgery. My mind was soon set to rest.

One day I was in the children's ward talking to a young couple about their child who had just been admitted with severe burns. I was telling them about the treatment, about the skin grafting, about the risks involved, and about the long hospitalization. They weren't interested. For one reason, it was a baby girl. For another, they didn't have the time or the money. Then I noticed the new sweeper; he'd been cleaning the bathroom and had overheard our conversation. Even if I had been disposed to pressure the couple to stay, which I was not, I would have had difficulty doing so with the sweeper in earshot. Finally I suggested they take the child home and went to write the discharge. A few minutes later, the sweeper came up and pulled at my sleeve. "They'll stay," he said. "I convinced them."

He smiled at me knowingly. It seemed he had more faith in our treatment than I had. The doctor no longer knew best.

Favorite Bus Rides

T *HE UNBROKEN LINE* of flimsy wooden shops and hotels extended a quarter of a mile down either side of the road. Beyond the hot tin roofs, the distant hills shimmered in the haze. The road swarmed with laughing children clad only in ragged shirts. Up and down the shop fronts trudged sturdy porters bent beneath the heavy loads they had carried down from the surrounding hills to barter or sell. It was 1976. This was Dumre, a bustling town on the new east-west highway, eighty miles west of Kathmandu. Four years earlier when the road was built, Dumre consisted of only a few thatched huts. Now it was the trading hub for hundreds of villages scattered over the Himalayan foothills north and south of the highway, including Amp Pipal, fifteen miles to the north.

Dumre was a picture of the kind of development that occurs when a new road winds its way through wild and previously roadless country. Littering the landscape were kerosene and diesel drums, mounds of rock salt hauled in from Tibet by mule train, signs everywhere advertising Star Beer, cold drinks, Himal Cigarettes, family planning, and "modern" hotels with "Himalayan view," rusting, wrecked pre-World War II vehicles that seemed to have expired in the very effort of establishing this outpost of civilization, and empty cartons, bottles, and tin cans of every description.

Inside the uniform rows of unpainted shops were goods ranging from immense copper caldrons to Annapurna Aromatic Incense Sticks.

A sharp clanking, rattling sound gradually intruded upon the monotonous tapping, banging, scraping noises of the town. The Kathmandu Express Bus came into sight and grated to a stop before a large and impatient crowd. A solid mass of humanity was jammed inside the bus, while on top at least thirty more people sat huddled together between sacks and boxes. One hundred and fifty individuals were packed into and onto that rickety fifty-five passenger vehicle, an antiquated relic handed down to the Mahendra Transport Company of Nepal after twenty-five years of rough service on the roads of India. The garish paintings of Hindu deities and the brightly colored geometric patterns that festooned the bus did little to conceal its dilapidated condition.

The driver, a beardless lad of eighteen, amused himself by repeatedly blowing the horn, the one part of the bus still in its prime. A few individuals trying to get off the bus, fought their way through the crowd struggling to get on. Twenty people clambered to the top, some with trunks and large bedrolls; another dozen clung to the ladders on the back of the bus. I managed to squeeze inside and find just enough room to stand upright by the back door. Within three minutes of its arrival, the bus groaned out of Dumre toward Kathmandu, and I was on my way to the very first meeting of the Health Services Board of the United Mission to Nepal.

One of the more onerous, nonetheless indispensable, tasks in any mission organization is administration. Fortunately some have gifts and inclinations in that direction. But for those of us who do not, sitting through three days of meetings is about as congenial as having the mumps.

As the medical director of Amp Pipal Hospital, one of the

United Mission's four hospitals in Nepal, I was expected to attend the meetings of the Health Services Board (HSB), whose function was to formulate the medical plans and policies of the United Mission.

Going to the meetings wouldn't have been so bad if I had had nothing better to do. But the five or six days spent going to the HSB three times a year were a considerable and unwelcome disruption of my busy daily schedule of caring for patients who, in my absence, had no other surgeon.

I recall the inaugural meeting of the HSB in February of 1976. My suggestion that someone else attend in my place had not been warmly received; I had been obliged to attend. Since the HSB had just been formed and this was our maiden meeting, we spent most of the time getting organized. Attending that first meeting was a heady experience. Important proposals were being weighed and decided, and the course of the mission's medical work was charted into the future.

But by the second meeting, the charm had worn away. The major part of subsequent meetings was spent approving budgets and deliberating over such mundane matters as job descriptions, appointments, and rules of employment. Often the smaller and seemingly less consequential items generated the most discussion: whether the toilet facilities of a small building in one of the projects should be outdoors or indoors; why the Amp Pipal Hospital needed five new mattresses (five had been stolen), what kind they should be, and whether they should be purchased from the recurring budget or the capital budget. Even our request for a new chain for our chain saw was discussed. After long and heated deliberation, our request was denied because a chain saw was not "appropriate technology" for a developing country like Nepal. Our builder, who had made the request and who knew more about appropriate technology than anyone on the board, later received a replacement chain as a gift from his brother in Canada.

During another planning session, we hotly debated whether the goal of our hospitals over the next five years should be to eradicate ninety-nine percent of intestinal parasites or only fifty percent. Since we had little hope of eliminating even five percent, the argument was immaterial. The optimists won in the end, and the one percent of parasites "allowed to survive" was the only concession granted to reality.

True, there were difficulties: the practice of calling fifteen busy medical workers into Kathmandu for three days of meetings was cumbersome, and the appropriateness of giving a central board responsibility for making even minute decisions for a dozen disparate and far-flung projects was questionable.

But despite these drawbacks, the balance of the HSB sessions were helpful and illuminating. Furthermore, a unity of spirit and purpose consistently emerged that was a testimony to both the strength and the uniqueness of the United Mission to Nepal.

My most vivid recollections, however, are not of the HSB meetings themselves, but of the time spent in getting to them and back again. The fifteen-mile walk down the mountain to Dumre was invariably the most refreshing part of the trip. It provided the mental and physical conditioning necessary to survive the grueling six-hour bus ride along the tortuous one-lane highway to Kathmandu.

My first crowded bus ride set the pattern for those that followed. On only three of my fourteen trips to HSB meetings, did I find a regular seat for any more than a small part of the journey.

On the second trip, I had the misfortune of being compressed through the front door of the bus into a packed line of passengers standing in the aisle. I barely had space on the floor for all ten of my toes. After half an hour, I noticed that no one was sitting on the motor casing, right up front in the middle. It looked inviting, so I sat on it.

The May day was hot, and the overcrowded bus, carrying at least three times its recommended load, did poorly on the hills, laboring jerkily upward in the lowest gear. On each uphill grade, the motor overheated, as did the clever fellow sitting on the motor casing. More people had jammed into the bus, so I was unable to get off the motor. Just when I thought I could stand it no longer, we would reach the top of the grade and the fresh breeze from outside would enter the bus as it picked up speed going downhill. I enjoyed only momentary relief, however, because as soon as we reached bottom, the sequence repeated itself as we began to ascend the next hill. If a fried egg had feelings, I'd know what they were.

Fortunately for me, the bus never made it to the final twenty-mile hill leading up to Kathmandu. Shortly before we reached it, the bus lurched to a stop with a terrific rasping and grinding noise arising from the transmission directly under my feet. After a six-hour wait, another bus arrived from Kathmandu to retrieve us. We reached our destination a little after midnight.

Some of the regular seats I have sat in have not been any better. On the third trip, I again tried the rear of the bus, getting a seat in the very back corner. When sufficient passengers had crowded aboard to prevent me from changing my place, I looked down at my feet and noticed a large part of the floor was missing. The consequence of this I soon discovered: Each time the bus encountered an unpaved section of road, dust shot up through the floor in great clouds and enveloped me from head to foot.

After that I learned to be wary of empty seats. Most buses had at least one. At each stop a rush of people would try to claim the vacant space until it was found, as was usually the case, that the previous occupant had been sick to his stomach.

On another occasion I rode into Kathmandu with Ken Webster, our project business manager. Ken was a former department store executive from Australia, newly arrived in Nepal. We were pleasantly surprised to get two seats together when we boarded the bus at Dumre, and with Ken fastidiously dressed in a white shirt and tie, I felt as if I were traveling in executive style.

At the next stop, a man with a very large goat got on the bus and squeezed himself down next to Ken, with the goat in between them. The goat wore a lugubrious expression. A long white Ho Chi Minh beard—goatee—trailed from the animal's chin, which rested comfortably on Ken's left knee. The goat was our traveling companion (or rather Ken's) for the next four hours. Not once did Ken look down at the goat or in any way acknowledge its existence. But when he ate the lunch his wife had prepared for him, I noticed the curious way he held the paper bag right up next to his chin and slid the contents surreptitiously out of the bag and into his mouth. The goat rolled its eyes and salivated copiously on Ken's trousers.

Ken should have been grateful the goat had its face toward him. One of Ken's countrywomen, a dignified gray-haired pediatrician who had worked for some years at Amp Pipal, also shared a seat with a goat once. The animal, however, was not facing her. The bus took a couple of very bad bumps and, before she knew what had happened, the goat had urinated into her traveling bag. She couldn't use the bag again for months, she claimed, because of the smell.

Occasionally the HSB meetings were held in Tansen, a large town to the southwest of Amp Pipal where the United Mission ran a 100-bed hospital. The trip by bus was longer and more involved, usually requiring two days and a change of buses in Pokhara. On one such trip I arrived in Pokhara just in time to see the Tansen Express Bus pull onto the highway and head south. But at least I would be the first customer for the next bus and have my choice of seat, a rare privilege.

The next bus was not an express bus, although when I asked if it were, I was told, "Yes, yes. Express bus, yes." They call anything "express" if that's what it takes to get you on board. I got on. After contemplating my seating choices, I decided to sit behind the driver because of an extra foot and a half of floor space. In most other seats, the average Westerner has to ride in the fetal position. Long before we started, however, my extra foot space shrunk to nothing. Soon it was crammed with other people's boxes and baggage, including some things of the driver's, and by the time we were off, there was hardly even space for my feet.

I found myself confronting a worse problem. Attached to the frame above the driver's seat and facing me was a small loudspeaker I had failed to notice. Only after two plump Nepali women had wedged themselves into the two feet of empty seat next to me and the bus was filled and ready to go, did the speaker suddenly come to life. It was wired to a cassette recorder on which the driver played his favorite Indian and Nepali music. Since the speaker faced away from the driver, he had to turn the volume on full to distinguish the music from the roar of the motor. Compared to the racket produced by the speaker, however, the sound of the motor was like the purr of a cat.

The driver owned four tapes, all heavy on percussion,

which we listened to for the entire nine-hour journey to Tansen. Midway through the trip a drunk singer provided a diversion when he boarded the bus and sang at the top of his lungs for almost an hour before falling asleep—beaten out by the tape recorder.

The combination of gasoline fumes, Indian rock music, hairpin curves, and general exhaustion left me barely able to stand when I finally stumbled off the bus hours later in Tansen. The first day of meetings was a dead loss, and I wasn't myself again until it was time to take the bus back to Amp Pipal.

The worst trip by far, however, was a return trip from Kathmandu. I was accompanied by two nurses: one, a British woman, was the director of our community health program; the other was our American operating-room supervisor. We had reserved our seats in advance on an express bus that left early in the morning. The bus, the swiftest available, was a short, squat vehicle, specially designed to take curves with no reduction in speed.

Negotiating the first twenty switchbacks down the long descent out of Kathmandu in the semidarkness was like taking a bobsled run in a high-speed orange crate. After twenty more switchbacks, my stomach was squeezing the oranges. By the sixtieth curve, my head was out the window, and before we were down the mountain, I had discharged alongside the bus everything I had eaten during the three days of meetings. And four more hours of winding, mountainous road remained ahead of us.

By the time we reached Dumre, I was unable to get off the bus and was beyond caring. My friends dragged me out of my seat, and several Nepali passengers solicitously carried my few articles of luggage. The driver, relieved that the risk of my expiring under his charge had passed, came around to the door of the bus to see that I was safely off.

"It's the Amp Pipal doctor," murmured a small crowd of townspeople to one another as they clustered around to witness my unprofessional emergence from the bus. The operating-room supervisor kept insisting that I "stand up and walk"; I had the feeling I was embarrassing her before all these onlookers. It may have been, however, that she was merely enjoying this reversal of our usual roles. In any event, I was incapable of following her instructions.

No one questioned my inability to hike fifteen miles, however, so two stout porters, both of them old acquaintances, were hired to carry me in a basket that had one side cut away for my legs to hang out. Some time was spent settling me into the basket so I wouldn't fall out or become otherwise discomposed, and much unsolicited advice was offered by the townspeople who had come to see us off. I had become a basket case.

A steady downpour enlivened the first part of our journey by making the trail slick and treacherous. The operating-room supervisor held an umbrella over me whenever the trail was wide enough to accommodate her ample frame beside the basket. Along the way, wide-eyed villagers looked out of doorways and shops.

"It's the Amp Pipal doctor," one would say.

"No, it couldn't be."

"Yes, it is. I recognize him for sure."

"What's wrong with him?"

"Don't know."

"He got sick on the bus," our spare carrier would explain helpfully.

"No. Really?"

"Is that all that's wrong with him?"

"Yes. Vomited all the way from Kathmandu, they say."

It was an undignified malady; I might have wished for

almost any other. But at the time I didn't care. I was finally learning why so many of our patients told us they would rather die than come to the hospital in a basket.

The most unpleasant part of the ride was the rhythmic jouncing of the basket at each step of the carrier. This was cruelly aggravated by the operating-room supervisor who kept force-feeding me with water as if her reward in heaven depended on the volume of fluid she poured down my throat. I could actually hear the water sloshing in my stomach and I feared I might do to the back of my carrier what I had done to the side of the bus. I was spared that further mortification, however, and eventually, after six hours of slogging through the mud in a drizzling rain, we arrived at a small village near the foot of Liglig Mountain. Here we stayed for the night.

By morning my terrible nausea had mostly gone, but I was still too weak to walk—especially up a mountain. Toward noon, however, I began to recover my strength. The discomfort of the basket had gradually exceeded my disinclination to walk, and I managed to finish the last two hours of the journey on my own feet. Several cups of sweet tea completed my rejuvenation, and I concluded the day and most of the evening by performing five operations on patients who had "piled up" during my five-day absence. After seven more operations the next day, we were caught up with the backlog, and another meeting of the HSB had come and gone.

Whenever I think of that last bus ride, I think how lucky I was to have had a seat by the window. Of all the dismaying aspects of bus sickness, none can be more dreadful than having nowhere to throw up. Such was once the case with Rigmor Hildershavn, our attractive blonde Norwegian nursing superintendent, on one of her bus rides into Kathmandu. Being prone to motion sickness, she decided to ride on top of the bus where the fresh air and open space might keep her stomach calm. A couple of stops later, a large group of students returning to school after a holiday joined her on top of the bus. She counted over fifty of them. Soon she was completely walled in by a press of young men, back-to-back and knee-to-knee, a princess surrounded by her court. As the lone female among a crowd of young males, Rigmor was the center of attraction, exciting the curiosity and admiration of those around her.

Then she began to feel sick. She could not get to the edge of the bus, so she prayed that the bus would stop to pick up a passenger. But it didn't; it was full. Then she remembered her sandwiches that were in a plastic container in her pack. Taking out the container, she broke up the sandwiches and nonchalantly tossed the pieces one by one into the air, as if she were feeding sea gulls from the upper deck of a ferryboat. When the last piece was overboard, she threw up into the plastic container, replaced the lid, and carefully put it back into her pack. A hush fell upon the top of the bus. Who can guess the thoughts of Rigmor's fifty awe-stricken admirers?

Govinda Devkota

*T*HE HSB MEETINGS have been hard not only on the board members; they have caused hardships for others as well. For this reason my participation at the HSB meetings will be forever linked in my mind with the story of Govinda Devkota, a middle-aged Brahmin farmer who lived in a village on the other side of Liglig Mountain, a two-hour walk from the hospital.

Brahmins fare poorly in the estimation of many Westerners. They are considered proud and overbearing, disdainful, and self-righteous. They are the wealthy class, owning the best land, exploiting the landless farmers who work for them (the landowner gets one half of the crop and does none of the work), and oppressing the poor by loaning them desperately needed cash and then taking their land when they can't pay the money back.

In spiritual matters, too, Brahmins enjoy preeminence. They serve as the priests of Hinduism, and even those who are not technically trained as priests serve unofficially in that capacity, especially in the smaller villages. Many times I have seen a low-caste Nepali stoop to kiss the foot of a rich Brahmin. The act is performed perfunctorily, without evident resentment. For the stooped Nepali, it is his karma (fate). For the Brahmin, it is his due.

This portrait of the average Brahmin is probably based on

fact, as are many stereotypes, but I have met very few Brahmins who fit the picture. And I know many who are completely the opposite; such was Govinda Devkota.

Govinda, first of all, was not rich; he was barely middle-class. He had no tenant farmers; he worked his own land; no one kissed his feet. He sent his two sons to school at great sacrifice. He had taken no second or third wife, a common practice among those who could afford such luxuries, but had remained faithful and devoted to his first wife. He was serious-minded yet kindly, humble, and always good-natured. Indeed he possessed the qualities that have so endeared Nepalis to me: honesty, simplicity, and reliability. I had liked and respected Govinda from the first day I met him during our third year in Amp Pipal.

He was lying on my examining table when I first saw him. For several weeks he had been troubled by pains in his stomach, mostly on the right side. In the past few days, the pain had become much worse and spread throughout his abdomen. He had lost faith in the usual village remedies; all the prescribed sacrifices had been carried out, and even the village priest was at a loss.

Finally Govinda called his family together and told them to take him to the new mission hospital at Amp Pipal. A few people from the village had been to the hospital for routine ailments and were helped, but no one had yet gone with anything serious. A few of the village elders objected. They said the hospital was *not* the place to take someone so sick, that people had actually died after going there. They suggested instead that a well-known shaman be called from a neighboring town. But Govinda would not hear of it; he had made up his mind to go to the hospital even though he had never been there himself and had no way of knowing what would happen to him once he got there. So early that morning, Govinda had been carried to Amp Pipal in a basket. I found him lying in my office, surrounded by his anxious family and half a dozen skeptical neighbors.

Though in severe pain, Govinda was alert and courteous throughout my questioning. He looked sick enough, but only when I examined his abdomen did I realize just how sick he really was. He had generalized peritonitis; his entire abdomen was swollen and tender. He was dehydrated; his pulse was weak; his breathing was rapid and shallow. He had not eaten in weeks, he said, because it made the pain worse. He had lost a lot of weight and, from the looks of him, he had started with little to spare. He needed emergency surgery, but he was an extremely poor operative risk. I had been at Amp Pipal three years, but I still thought twice about operating on critically ill patients; if too many died, our work could be set back years, decades.

When I mentioned the need for surgery, Govinda's family threw up their hands and said they were taking him home at once; they had only come for some medicine. But again Govinda overruled them. "I'm staying here," he told them, "and if the doctor says I need an operation, I shall agree to it." I liked him for that. "Besides," he added, "what have I got to lose?"

He was right, he had nothing to lose; he was going to die without surgery and he knew it. Only the hospital and I stood to lose if he died: One more death would be added to our account.

We carried out the usual preoperative preparation: intravenous fluids, antibiotics, a stomach tube, a urinary catheter. My tentative diagnosis was a ruptured gall bladder, with spillage of bile into the peritoneal cavity, a rare condition that is almost always fatal if not surgically corrected. A perforated stomach ulcer or a ruptured appendix would have been a far more common cause for the patient's physical findings, but his symptoms fit neither of those ailments. In this case, as with most abdominal emergencies, the first and foremost decision is whether or not to operate. Making the precise diagnosis was secondary and usually easy once the incision was made. In Govinda's case, the first decision was easy: an operation was essential.

When I made the incision in his abdomen, the first thing to greet my eyes was a gush of turbid-green fluid that surged over the edge of the wound onto the drapes and down onto the floor. It was indeed a ruptured gall bladder, and it was so embedded in adhesions that I could hardly find it. The best I could do under the circumstances was to run a tube from the gall bladder through the abdominal wall to the outside in order to drain off the bile. The tube would stay in place as long as bile continued to drain. If Govinda survived, I would remove his gall bladder at a later date when its removal would be less dangerous.

Govinda not only survived, he recovered more quickly than any of us thought possible. I removed the tube within a few days of his surgery; his wound healed rapidly; his pain disappeared. Ten days after his operation, he walked home, a grateful patient. I warned him that he would have repeated attacks of cholecystitis (inflammation of the gall bladder), but he never had even one. In fact I never had to remove his gall bladder.

A few months passed before Govinda came back to the hospital. The moment I spotted him, I said to myself, *Oh no, his gall bladder is acting up.* But he hadn't come for himself. He had brought a man from his village who needed treatment but who was hesitant to come on his own. After that I saw Govinda at the hospital regularly, perhaps five or six times a year. He always came for the same reason: to bring a sick person who otherwise would have been afraid to come to the hospital. If someone he brought had to be hospitalized, Govinda would help with the arrangements, even to the point of staying in the hospital with the patient until a member of the family could be summoned. His faith in our ability to cure even the most desperate illnesses made him the best salesman we ever had. More than a salesman, he was a living advertisement.

But one day almost seven years after his operation, Govinda again became ill. Severe crampy pains suddenly began radiating throughout his abdomen. He knew the consequences of delaying, so the very next morning he arrived at the hospital. He was in early intestinal obstruction and would need emergency surgery. There was just one problem. Only two hours earlier, I had left for yet another meeting of the HSB.

In rural Nepal, patients seldom come to the hospital quickly. This tendency to delay going to the hospital is particularly noticeable in cases of intestinal obstruction, perhaps because the results of waiting are so disastrous. These patients suffer incredible agonies. At the insistence of well-meaning friends and relatives, they often remain at home until the many village nostrums have been exhausted. All the while they become more and more bloated, dehydrated, and weakened. Finally after being carried a one or two days' journey to the hospital, they arrive in such precarious condition that surgery is frequently out of the question. If we do operate to relieve the obstruction, they often succumb, either during the surgery or during the first few postoperative days.

My friend Govinda, however, had not delayed; he had come at once. For him an operation would have entailed little risk and almost certainly would have been successful. But I was gone. The medical doctors on duty, in accordance with a prearranged plan for handling surgical emergencies in my absence, sent Govinda to the 100-bed government hospital in Pokhara—a fifteen-mile trek to Dumre and then a three-hour bus ride. Getting sick was bad enough, but to have to go to an unknown, far-off city to be treated by total strangers was almost as bad again, not to mention the extra expenses. Because the mother could not manage the journey alone, the older son would have to interrupt his studies to accompany his parents. They had to decide quickly; precious hours were slipping away. In the end they knew they had only one choice.

Procuring carriers and making the necessary arrangements was not possible on such short notice, so Govinda spent that day in the Amp Pipal Hospital receiving intravenous fluids and pain medication. Early the next morning he was taken down the mountain in a *doli* (a hammock suspended from either end of a long, sturdy pole carried on the shoulders of two men). The suffering he endured along the way can scarcely be imagined: the intense spasms of pain, the repeated vomiting, the swollen abdomen, the hot sun, the crowded bus.

When Govinda reached the hospital in Pokhara that night, the surgeon was not there. He was on "casual leave" and was not expected back until the next day. When he had not appeared on the second day, staff members told the family he would surely arrive the following day. When the third day came and went with still no surgeon, even the hospital staff lost their assurance that he would return soon. Meanwhile the patient was becoming progressively debilitated and dispirited. The pain and vomiting had become unbearable. On the morning of the fourth day, Govinda demanded to be taken back to Amp Pipal.

"My surgeon will be back from Kathmandu tonight," he said. "He will take care of me first thing tomorrow."

So that same morning, just as I was leaving Kathmandu, Govinda and his family left Pokhara.

The bus journey from Pokhara was shorter, so Govinda and his wife and son arrived in Dumre some hours ahead of me. After hiring carriers and a doli, at a price that would exceed their entire hospital bill, they started on the trail to Amp Pipal. I caught up with them in the late afternoon near the top of Liglig Mountain. Govinda was so emaciated that I hardly recognized him. Furthermore I could not understand why he was being carried to the hospital along this trail, since I knew his house to be in another direction. Govinda could scarcely speak, but his eyes lit up with hope the moment he saw me. I listened in disbelief as his son told me all that had happened. One look at the cadaverous form told me he was too far gone for surgery, but when I mentioned my thought to the son, he immediately cried out, "You've got to operate! He was this sick before, and you saved him. We've come all the way back here just for this. You've got to give him a chance."

The sick man said faintly, "I don't care if I die from the surgery. Even if I have only the tiniest chance to live, please operate. I believe you can heal me."

"Only God can heal you," I said. *If God is planning a miracle, does He want it done with surgery or without,* I wondered to myself.

All through that night, Govinda received bottle after bottle of intravenous fluid and high doses of antibiotics, along with great infusions of hope and encouragement from the hospital staff on duty.

Govinda was only slightly less moribund in the morning, but all agreed we should go ahead with surgery. Our first hurdle was inducing anesthesia, a procedure that can cause the demise of critically ill patients, especially when it is administered by marginally trained staff in a minimally equipped rural hospital. Govinda, however, was anesthetized without difficulty. Since a patient's tolerance of anesthesia is often a good indication of how well he will tolerate surgery, we began to hope, ever so faintly, that maybe he would make it after all. On opening the abdomen, however, all hope vanished. Ugly red-black, distended coils of intestine slithered endlessly up out of the incision, accompanied by liters of dark, foul-smelling fluid. We resected fifteen feet of necrotic bowel and sutured together the ends of what was left. Incredibly the patient remained stable throughout this horrendous procedure. As we began to close the abdomen, our short-lived optimism returned, at first tentatively, but then with growing intensity. We praised God for what was clearly His protection over Govinda Devkota's life. I anticipated the joy of telling his wife and son that the operation had been successful and that his chances for recovery were good.

We were sewing the skin when the Nepali anesthetist announced that the patient's blood pressure had dropped. We turned off the ether and poured in intravenous fluids and plasma expander. We checked everywhere to discover a correctable cause for this sudden reversal in Govinda's condition. We found none. He deteriorated rapidly and died as we were putting on the dressing. The cause of death was septic shock, a complication frequently fatal even in medical centers in the West. His wife and two daughters, who had just arrived from home, set up a wailing that could be heard all over the hospital and much of the hillside. Govinda's death was a sad end to a life that had been an important part of our hospital ministry over many years. It was also the first death we knew of that was the direct result of my participation in the HSB. With renewed vigor, I pleaded to be allowed to send someone else in my place in the future.

Nirmala

*W*HEN THE NEXT HSB MEETING was scheduled, a special administrative matter requiring my presence was on the agenda. Since no catastrophes occurred during my absence this time, my attendance at future meetings began again to seem both tolerable and reasonable. What happened to Govinda Devkota had been a fluke; such a thing could not occur twice.

So several months later when it came time for the next HSB session (the second since Govinda Devkota's tragedy), I packed my knapsack, dusted off my shoes, and set out on the trail for Dumre. Unfortunately my sanguine predictions did not come true. On the second day of the meetings as I dozed in my cushioned seat, the person next to me nudged my elbow and pointed to someone at the door who was trying to get my attention. It was the "headman" of the small village nearest our hospital. He had come by bus to Kathmandu to give me an urgent letter from my colleague Dr. Helen Huston. Helen had written that the headman's daughter Nirmala had suddenly become seriously ill with a painful enlarging mass in her lower abdomen and that I should leave the meetings immediately and return to Amp Pipal to operate on her.

The father, distraught and tired from his journey and from two sleepless nights at the hospital tending his daughter, waited until I had finished reading the letter and then pleaded with me to return to Amp Pipal without delay. Since I had already accomplished what little administrative business I had come to do, I was free to leave at once. When I told the father I would go with him, he grinned appreciatively through his week-old white bristles. There was no doubt that he cherished his daughter deeply.

I knew both Nirmala and her father well. I also knew her mother, her older sister, and younger brother; I had treated every member of her family. Some years before, the older sister had nearly died from taking a local worm medicine, a potent concoction that occasionally killed people along with the worms and was available for the asking in almost every village. Three years earlier I had operated on Nirmala's mother for a twisted ovarian cyst, from which she had recovered uneventfully. A year later, while cutting firewood on the steep north side of Liglig Mountain, she fell twenty or thirty feet off a cliff, breaking her neck. This damaged her spinal cord and left her paralyzed on the right side of her body and numb on the left. For weeks she lay on the front porch of her house in constant pain, showing no sign of improvement. Then some of the Christians on the hospital staff started to pray with her, and her condition began to improve. Within a year she had only a slight limp and some tingling in her left foot to remind her of her narrow escape.

The father was one of the first Nepalis we became acquainted with in Amp Pipal. Although he was busy as one of the foremen in charge of building the hospital, he was happy to do work around our house in his spare time. He built our workshed, made a stone stairway so we could walk instead of slide down the hill below our house, and terraced our garden. He was a boisterous, cantankerous individual, a former Gurkha soldier, always proud to tell anyone who would listen all about his wound. But despite his rough manner and hot temper, he commanded the respect and grudging admiration of his fellow-villagers. And he could get a job done faster than anyone else, even if it took banging a few heads together to do so.

Nirmala was his prize and pride. She was a beautiful young woman of about twenty-five, self-possessed, gracious, and bright. She was married to a Gurkha soldier stationed in Singapore, who came home on leave once every two years. She had enrolled in our first class for assistant nurses in 1971; now in 1980, she was one of our most capable Nepali staff members. Nirmala's position pleased her father greatly: Getting his daughter a prestigious full-time job at the new hospital had been one of his major goals, not because the family needed the money but because it gave him an edge in his fierce and longstanding rivalry with the *other* headman of the village, with whom he continually competed for power and influence. Nirmala's employment at the hospital had infuriated this other headman, who couldn't rest until he had seen his own daughter—even more lovely than Nirmala—safely admitted to the next class for assistant nurses. Their score was even—for the moment.

For all her beauty and talent, Nirmala had one grave defect: She was a kleptomaniac. This flaw overshadowed all her virtues. We hadn't known it when we hired her; she had picked up this compulsion from her parents. Her father, we heard, used to fill his *topi* (cap) at the end of each workday with hospital cement and then prop it back on his head and stroll carefully home. In two months he had accumulated enough cement to plaster the outside of his house—the only house in his village so distinguished. Everyone, it seemed, knew about it but us.

We first caught Nirmala stealing medicine, and we promptly suspended her. How that other headman gloated! He let it be known that *his* daughter would never do anything like that. Nirmala's father was enraged and threatened us with dire consequences if Nirmala was not reinstated. He rallied his supporters in the panchayat to put pressure on us. The followers of the other headman rallied in our defense; the entire community took sides. Nirmala's husband, who happened to be home on leave, felt particularly disgraced and vowed vengeance on our Indian laboratory technician, the person who had reported Nirmala's theft. One day as the lab technician was walking to work, the husband accosted him with a gun and threatened to kill him. He likely would have done so except for the timely arrival of Tej, the laundryman, who attacked the husband from behind and wrested his gun away. All this excitement was too much for the Indian lab technician, however, who left us shortly thereafter and never returned.

Meanwhile our nursing superintendent at the time, a stern and resolute Scottish missionary named Mabel McLean, refused to bow to pressure or threats. Mabel would not have been intimidated by Saint George's dragon, much less by Nirmala's father. So the father, sensing he was getting nowhere, switched to cajolery. This evidently worked better, because six months later Nirmala got her job back.

Unfortunately she had not reformed; she was just craftier. Only after several years did we realize that she was filching hospital supplies on an almost daily basis. But we could never catch her. Finally in desperation, we laid a trap for her; she obliged us by falling into it. A pen was all we caught her stealing, but it was enough. We gave her the option of resigning quietly, and she took it. But her father flew into a fury when he heard about it. After making a public scene at the hospital for over an hour, he announced he was going up to break apart the hospital's large stone water tank, which he himself had built years earlier. "What I've built for these swindlers, I can tear down just as easily!" he shouted as he stormed off. And he proceeded to do exactly what he had said—in broad daylight.

What concerned us most was not the damage to the water tank, but the likelihood that such a brazen assault on hospital property, if unpunished, would unleash a host of similar attacks. Already we were troubled by minor acts of vandalism, usually committed by disgruntled villagers who could not get work at the hospital. So we decided to take strong action against Nirmala's father, reasoning that if we punished a leader in the village for wrongdoing, maybe the lesser offenders would take note and stop troubling us. As medical director, I was appointed to send for the police to come and arrest Nirmala's father. This they did with dispatch and with gratifying results. Not only did the vandalism stop, but Nirmala's father, now subdued and even contrite, publicly apologized and promised to repair the damaged tank at his own expense. After he had done so, I was to inspect his work and then send him back to the police station with a letter certifying that the job had been done to my satisfaction. For this proud and pugnacious man, such an experience was humiliating. It was softened, however, by the inability of his rival headman to take full advantage of his downfall. Not long before, the other man's own daughter had disgraced herself and her family by abruptly quitting her job at the hospital and running away with a married man of lower caste. Such are the trials of being a headman in a Nepali village.

The friendship between Nirmala's father and me was actually reinforced, not ruptured, by these events, and our respect for one another, if anything, increased. We remained wary of each other, but no further strains tested our relationship. For a long time after that, he kept begging me, almost weekly, to reinstate Nirmala. Although I was sympathetic, our nurses would hear nothing of it. He stopped asking eventually, and Nirmala never worked for us again— to my deep regret, I might add, and undoubtedly to hers.

Now, three years later, I was being given the chance to show this father and his daughter a special kindness. I wouldn't have missed it for anything.

Already the time was two o'clock, however, and we had no way of getting to Amp Pipal that day. The last bus for Dumre had already left. I did not know whether Nirmala would survive if we waited until the next morning to catch the bus. After consulting with some of our United Mission people, we learned that the site manager for the construction of the new 150-bed hospital near Kathmandu had access to a jeep and would be happy to drive us to Dumre after work. Without hesitation, we accepted his offer.

We left Kathmandu at five o'clock. The site manager, a Canadian named Tom Haggerty, brought his wife along on the outing. With me was an unexpected visitor, a writer I had never met. He had arrived in Kathmandu only the day before and had asked to accompany me to Amp Pipal. Nirmala's father, usually talkative, was as taciturn as a mummy.

As we wound our way down the twenty-mile hill from Kathmandu, we could see the long line of Himalayas stretching to the west, silhouetted against the setting sun. Seventy miles away rose Himalchuli, a giant Matterhorn and nearly twice as high. Somewhere near its base was Amp Pipal. Further to the west lay the fortresslike Annapurna massif, and still further on was the southern end of the Dhaulagiri range, a dark outline in the reddening haze. Three thousand feet below, twilight had spread along the valley floor and was reaching up to meet us as we descended. In the deepening gloom, we could discern the flickering lights of a thousand cooking fires. It was the end of a day, but for us it seemed more like the beginning. The road pitched and twisted on and on into the night.

We arrived in Dumre at ten-thirty and then proceeded bumpily up the new jeep track that led almost to the foot of Liglig Mountain. The trail had only recently been hacked out with pick and shovel by the villagers living in the vicinity. It saved us one half of the walking distance—the easy half—but only an hour's time. The road was so rough that a vehicle could barely go faster than someone on foot. It would have been less wearing and far more pleasant to walk.

We reached the end of the jeep track at eleven-thirty. As the Haggertys turned their jeep around to return to Kathmandu, we started along the footpath to Amp Pipal. It was pitch dark.

My visitor, I discovered, had only a tiny penlight instead of the "good flashlight" I had told him to bring. He had come to Amp Pipal for adventure, but after he had slipped off the narrow, dew-moistened trail into knee-deep, mud-filled rice paddies half a dozen times, he had had enough for one night. When the trail actually began to ascend Liglig, it quickly became apparent that he wasn't in as good shape as he had thought; and the fact that he could see only four feet in front of him reinforced his impression that this mountain had no top. However, in spite of the slow pace occasioned by my companion's feeble legs and even feebler light, we reached our house by 3:30 A.M.—not bad time for the middle of a damp night. After settling my guest in bed, I went down to the hospital to examine Nirmala and see that the necessary arrangements were made for surgery first thing in the morning.

When I walked into Nirmala's room, her face relaxed for a moment in a smile of relief and gratitude. "Thank you for coming, doctor," she said faintly. "I knew you'd come. I prayed you would come. Thank you."

"Thank God, Nirmala, not me," I said. "He provided the vehicle to get us here and He has kept you alive until now. "And," I added, "He's going to see that you get well."

On purely medical grounds, I had little reason to be so confident. She was in a precarious state: Her entire lower abdomen was bulging with a tense, tender mass; her pulse was weak and rapid; her blood pressure hardly registered. I wondered if she, too, had a twisted ovarian cyst like her mother had had. Whatever it turned out to be, I knew our decision to return to Amp Pipal that night had been right. She could not have held out much longer.

At surgery a few hours later, we found that Nirmala did indeed have a gangrenous ovarian cyst about the size of a football. It was twisted three complete turns on its pedicle. Pulsating in the center of the necrotic pedicle was the big ovarian artery, ready to rupture. Nirmala recovered rapidly from her operation and walked home from the hospital seven days later.

The Flood

I WAS ASKED TO ATTEND only one more HSB meeting after that. Initially Dr. Helen had planned to go in my place, but an urgent matter arose that required both Cynthia and me to attend. I had to squeeze a week of surgery into the two days prior to leaving and then turn all the surgical patients over to Helen. This last-minute rush and the hectic turnover were always the worst part of going to HSB meetings—or anywhere else. And whichever doctor stayed behind was left with double the inpatients to care for, half of them unfamiliar, and an extra load in the outpatient clinic.

The night before we planned to leave, a child was brought to the hospital with a bad compound fracture of the forearm. The injury, already twenty-four hours old, required surgery in the morning. I had no choice but to stay and leave for the meetings one day late.

The following evening we busily packed for the trip to Kathmandu. No other surgical emergencies demanded my attention, and the hospital was uncommonly quiet. Being free of the hospital felt nice, and we were actually looking forward to the journey, especially now that most of the hassle and headache of leaving was behind us.

While we were packing, rain began to fall. This was not surprising as it was the end of the rainy season. It kept on raining, however, harder and harder all night and was still raining when we awoke in the morning. We had not experienced such a downpour here; elderly villagers said they had never seen such a rain. For twelve uninterrupted hours the water had come down in a steady deluge. We had planned to leave by 5 A.M. but it was almost seven o'clock before the rain eased enough for us to even step outside the house. We walked in the rain for six hours, all the way to Dumre. Sometimes it drizzled; sometimes it poured. The rain turned to mud from the knee down; rivulets of muddy water splashed and gurgled underfoot. Hardly a step landed securely, but thanks to the twisting and turning of the trail, we rarely slid more than a few feet at any one slip. A tiny creek partway down Liglig had become a waist-high torrent that we forded with unsteady, groping feet, while softball-sized rocks struck our legs as they hurtled downstream.

In the valley below Liglig, conditions were no better. Crossing the raised, narrow borders of the rice terraces was like walking along a greased pole laid over a sea of knee-deep sludge. Sometimes the trail disappeared completely into a broad, murky pond, through which we planted our feet with great care to avoid being upended. Once, hearing a loud splash behind me, I turned to see Cynthia sitting in the middle of one such pond; thereafter her backside was the subject of many giggles and comments as we went along.

Shortly after we reached Dumre, the rain ceased and the sun came out. As we waited for the bus, we noticed that all the vehicles passing through Dumre were going only in one direction—toward Kathmandu. None were coming *from* Kathmandu, nor had any come for most of the day, we learned. As we pondered the significance of the one-way traffic, our bus clanked into sight. To our wonder there were empty seats on the bus. We chose two front seats opposite the driver, remarking to one another that this promised to be the most pleasant trip we had yet taken to Kathmandu.

We casually mentioned to our driver that the road ahead might be blocked since no vehicles had come from Kathmandu all day. He merely shrugged and said he was sure he could get through. Besides, he had to be in Kathmandu that night anyway. Considering ourselves lucky to have so determined a driver, we settled back to enjoy the ride. The road followed a richly forested river valley. As we rode along, we could see numerous fresh landslides—the result of the night's rain— sharply etched on the surrounding hillsides. In several places, broad stretches of gravel and stones had washed across the road, sending the bus into paroxysms of shaking and rattling as we passed.

We had gone less than ten miles when suddenly we came upon a long row of vehicles lined up alongside the road: twenty buses, thirty or so trucks, and perhaps forty to fifty other cars and vans of various descriptions. Our driver uttered an oath, blasted his horn, and drove along the opposite side of the road, scattering the crowds of people who were walking to see the cause of the obstruction. Finally our driver could proceed no further and was obliged to pull over into an empty space behind another bus.

We all got out and walked to the head of the line. There the road ended. In its place was a wild and turbulent flood of water, forty yards wide, pouring across the highway. Uprooted trees swept past, and boulders the size of bass drums thumped downstream as if filled with air. The people milling near the water's edge—perhaps two thousand of them— moved from place to place, pointing, gesticulating, shouting in an effort to be heard over the deafening roar of the flood. No vehicles were on the other side of the torrent. That meant there was at least one other obstruction further up the road, and perhaps many more. Despite the determination of our driver, we would almost certainly not reach Kathmandu that day—maybe not even that week.

Our driver, impatient with waiting, was trying to round up his passengers by blowing his horn, as if our bus's horn could be distinguished from all the others that were by this time beeping and hooting. If he could not be the first to Kathmandu, he seemed determined to be the first back to Pokhara. As the last of our passengers was clambering aboard, he began to turn the bus around—no easy feat on a one-lane highway with other vehicles in front and back and deep ditches on either side.

After a few minutes of watching his violent exertions at the wheel and wondering when he would back us into the ditch, our attention was diverted by a loud rumbling noise coming down the road from Dumre. The noise was accompanied by a growing clamor of voices shouting, "The bozer! The bozer!" (the Nepali contraction for bulldozer). Actually it was a small Japanese loader, operated by a smiling, self-assured young man gaily outfitted in a multicolored topi and bright plaid scarf. He sat high in his tiny cab with the air of a raja riding his elephant. People scampered out of the way as the bozer rolled slowly forward. Our driver, having managed to turn our bus around only thirty degrees, suddenly abandoned the effort and pulled out after the bozer, following it right down the road to the head of the line. Meanwhile everyone once again poured out of the other buses, hailing the bozer with shouts of acclamation and running along after it to witness the anticipated struggle between man and nature—and its hoped-for outcome, the triumphant reopening of the road.

As it approached the flood, the bozer seemed to shrink in size. The breezy confidence of the young Nepali gradually disappeared as he surveyed the scene before him. Although the fury of the water had abated slightly, it was still awesome. Dozens of people climbed onto the bozer to offer their encouragement and advice. Hundreds of others clustered around yelling opinions into the air and jumping from boulder to boulder to gain the best view of the impending encounter. Foremost in the bozer driver's mind, I'm sure, was the thought of being swept downstream into the Indian Ocean. Nonetheless, goaded by the impatient exhortations of the crowd, the bozer driver started into the water. A great shout went up. The bozer looked like a Tonka toy propelled by an unseen hand as it pushed before it mounds of gravel and stones. At moments it seemed on the verge of being swallowed up by the water, which splashed halfway up its sides, as if angry at this intrusion on its right of way.

The bozer, however, was not swept downstream. Instead the young man at the controls set about in systematic fashion to clear the road. The task seemed endless: Each time a passage was cleared, it promptly filled up again with several feet of sand and rocks. Only after ten slow, tedious trips back and forth did the passageway begin to remain clear for more than a moment—time enough to allow one vehicle to slip through immediately in the wake of the bozer. Our bus driver and the driver of the bus at the head of the original line, which had arrived nine hours earlier, jockeyed to be first to cross. After maneuvering their buses back and forth and exchanging heated insults, the other driver outwitted ours. Pulling out after the bozer, he followed it across the torrent. The spectators watched with anxiety and excitement, expecting the bus at any moment to slide off the causeway and down the steep boulder-strewn embankment to the left. But the tires held; the engine didn't stall; and the bus reached the other side. The assembled multitude whooped and cheered as the bus drove triumphantly down the road to Kathmandu.

Back came the bozer, and it was our turn. Our driver revved up his engine and, with horn blaring, drove into the water, tailing the bozer by only a few inches. Twice the bozer operator waved furiously at our driver to allow a few feet of space between the vehicles; twice we stalled as the spray and foam washed up around the engine. Large rocks thudded against the side of the bus; mounds of sand piled up, threatening to block our progress. But we made it across. Near the other side, the bozer pulled off to the left to allow us to pass. As we roared out of the water, passengers on our bus erupted in cheers and clapping in honor of our intrepid driver and the various gods and goddesses that were considered to have delivered us from the angry flood. Perhaps we would get to Kathmandu after all.

But we had no sooner gotten onto dry land than a man standing in the middle of the road waving his arms brought both our bus and our cheers to an abrupt halt. He had walked, he said, from the next obstruction up the road: A bridge was out only five miles away that would take a month to repair. Besides, he added, there were no vehicles lined up on the far side of that washout either. There was no use going on. As this information was digested by the occupants of our bus, another bus appeared from the direction of Kathmandu. Our hopes were momentarily raised until we recognized it as the bus that had crossed ahead of us.

The news of the broken bridge was transferred across the water via the bozer, and after some time, we could see the long line of buses and trucks begin the tedious procedure of turning around and heading back to Pokhara. The bozer driver kept himself busy pushing stones and boulders here and there, and only when the sun was setting and almost all the other vehicles had gone, did he finally return to lead our bus and its deflated driver back across the water.

We spent the night in Dumre as guests of one of our tuberculosis patients. The next day, with not one cloud to give a moment's respite from the burning sun, we walked the six hours back up the mountain to Amp Pipal. No jeeps were running this time. The new jeep track was so badly washed away in so many places that it was weeks before it was passable again. When at last we arrived home, I told our startled colleagues that it had been the best HSB meeting I had ever attended.

That afternoon two surgical emergencies arrived at the hospital. Only then was I was truly thankful for the flood.

Others, however, had less to be thankful for. Dozens lost their lives and thousands lost their homes because of that flood. Most of the losses, as usual, were suffered by the very poor, who settle the landslide- and flood-prone land along the rivers and steeper slopes. Their houses are ill-constructed, with too much mud and too little stone, or perhaps with just bamboo slats interlaced with sticks and leaves. Such is Nepal: a land of many poor, of many floods, of many homes without foundations.

Our Finnish business manager, Esa Ahonen, went to the next HSB meeting, which was in Tansen. He wasn't any keener on going than I was, and his troubles began even before he left. He forgot to take a letter from Rigmor, our Norwegian nursing superintendent, requesting permission from the HSB to hire two urgently needed assistant nurses. (A new rule had gone into effect at the previous HSB meeting stipulating that no new staff members could be hired without the prior approval of the board.) Esa then managed to miss the chartered bus from Kathmandu to Tansen. He had expected to play a quiet, passive role at the meeting, but when he arrived, he was sharply challenged about why our new tuberculosis-leprosy wing at Amp Pipal was costing twice as much as originally planned. When the matter came up for a vote, however, Esa was inspired to point out that our entire 20-patient wing would cost only half as much as a single apartment in the staff residence the mission was building for its grand new hospital in the Kathmandu Valley. Our budget was passed without a murmur. Our business manager was indeed the right person to send to these meetings. We should have thought of it sooner.

chapter thirteen

Administrative Capers

M OST PEOPLE WHO BECOME missionaries have an adventuresome streak in them, a fascination with the unknown, a readiness to undertake things they were not prepared to do. It's good that they have, because very few missionaries know beforehand what they are actually getting into.

In one way, missionaries end up doing much less than they are trained to do; that is, they usually are not able to use all their technical skills in the countries to which they are sent. On the other hand, they frequently end up doing much more than they are trained to do, usually outside their own fields. We have all heard of doctors, teachers, and pastors who, as soon as they got to the mission field, of necessity became mechanics, builders, plumbers, dieticians, and marriage counselors—all wrapped into one. Jonathan Lindell, a teacher who came to Amp Pipal before the medical work began, not only taught subjects he had never taught, but he also became the village doctor, prescribing, as he told us once, aspirin for everything above the waist and diarrhea tablets for everything below. He had reduced the practice of medicine to its essentials.

A number of roles have been thrust on me over the years for which I had no prior training, experience, or inclination. One of these was the role of administrator. Sounds dull, to be sure, but administration in Amp Pipal is not what you think. Granted our operation is not complex—a little fifty-bed hospital, an annual operating budget of $10,000 at the outset (now almost $80,000), and a staff of sixty. It shouldn't require an M.B.A. to keep *that* going. However it's the hospital's location that makes the difference. Operating a hospital at the end of a fifteen-mile path in the Himalayan foothills is not a straightforward undertaking. In addition to the extracurricular activities such as bus rides and HSB meetings, there are numerous everyday (and equally diverting) problems that arise in the course of operating a "modern" institution in a very unmodern society—problems not dealt with in hospital management manuals.

Many of these problems center on the people we work with. Not only do our patients not know what to make of the hospital, neither do some of our staff. Most of our staff are Nepali villagers who live off the land. Some have passed third grade; others have studied through high school. The sweepers and cleaners are illiterate. Few have ever held jobs before, much less in a hospital, especially a foreign hospital. It's been a learning experience for everyone.

They have had all kinds of questions: How did one apply for a job at this new-fangled hospital? What was a work contract? Did they really have to arrive at work exactly at eight? Since most of them lived an hour away and some farther, they had to get up in the dark (especially in the winter months), bungle around to cook their rice (no one else eats at that hour), then walk to the hospital (rain, shine, or hail), and keep clean in the process. And how would they know when it was eight o'clock anyway? None of them had a watch. It was one of the first things they bought with their new wages, however: Our Scottish nursing superintendent was a stickler for punctuality. They might not have known exactly when it was eight, but they certainly knew when it was *after* eight, because Sister Mabel McLean would be there waiting for them.

Even I didn't escape the punctuality crunch. One day I came twenty minutes late for an afternoon operation—I had been trying to finish a grammar lesson. Sister Mabel stood in the operating-room entrance, arms folded, watch in hand.

"You're twenty minutes late."

"Yes, I know." (It wasn't the first time I'd been late.)

"I can't have this. My staff has been ready all this time, just waiting for you."

"Yes, I know."

"If you're late again, I won't allow you to schedule afternoon cases."

I would like to say that humility prevented me from retorting flippantly that she might like to do the surgery herself in that case, but it wasn't humility. It was just good sense. As the Bible says, if your adversary is greater than you, sue for peace quickly. A brief apology mollified Sister Mabel, and I was allowed to enter the operating room.

These young Nepali workers and one young American surgeon were banged into shape before they knew what hit them. After many years of nursing in Asia, Sister Mabel knew her business. She put the staff through a rigorous and first-rate training program that included—in addition to lessons on punctuality—anatomy, physiology, pathology, pharmacology, and nursing arts. They were issued snazzy new uniforms: plaid saris for the girls (a light touch of Scotland) and khakis for the boys. The boys could have two pairs of short pants in place of one pair of long pants if they liked. Going barefoot on duty was forbidden; most wore flip-flops.

Two classes of assistant nurses were graduated during Mabel's two years at Amp Pipal, and among them were some of the best hospital workers I have ever known. They were Mabel's miracles. They were always "her boys" and "her girls," and they were proud of it. I can imagine the ridicule such maternalism would generate in our modern orientation courses for missionaries. Treat nationals as equals, with respect—that is the word today. But that is exactly what Sister Mabel did. She treated them just as if she were back in Scotland and they were Scots. And that, when you think of it, is showing real respect. She turned them into proficient and self-confident adults, and she didn't do it by smiling wanly and wagging her head when they were derelict, as if they were retarded children. She treated them like young men and women, and that meant telling them where to get off when they needed it. And they respected her and grew to love her. Every mission hospital needs a Mabel McLean; so does every surgeon.

One of Sister Mabel's major accomplishments was teaching the staff to use toilets, a startling innovation in those early days. The staff was then to show the patients how to use them. This was less successful. The continuous influx of new people required daily initiations into the wonders of modern plumbing, and what had taken our staff weeks to digest could not be passed on to our patients in one lesson. And who was going to keep the toilets clean? The task was as monumental as it was repugnant. No village Nepali had ever been asked to do such a thing. The sweepers would do it, we decided, and anyone who signed on as a sweeper was made fully aware of this responsibility. But we never lacked for applicants for the job. Many villagers were so poor, so hungry, they would do anything for a salary of ten dollars a month.

There were worse jobs than cleaning toilets. One was burying dead bodies. For a Hindu, this task was so loathsome that we had to pay our sweepers a bonus for doing it—ten rupees (eighty cents) for a large body, five for a small one.

A still more objectionable duty was killing stray dogs. This job sounds unpleasant enough to Westerners, but to Hindus who believe in reincarnation it is close to murder. Yet we had no choice but to periodically eliminate the mangy, flea-bitten dogs that roamed the hospital wards scavenging for leftovers from the patients' pots and plates. We could tolerate one or two, but we drew the line at four or five. They trooped up and down the hospital corridors all day, fought and howled all night, and left their messes everywhere to be tracked around by feet oblivious to the dirty trails. The biggest concern the dogs caused, however, was the constant threat of rabies. Because of this danger, the panchayat gave us permission to kill stray dogs. His Majesty's government in Kathmandu sanctioned the activity as well. But when it came time to kill the first dog, we could find no one willing to do it.

This, too, was the sweepers' job, we had decided. I met with them to find a way to overcome their reluctance. I explained again the frightful danger of rabies; they all understood. I mentioned the dirt the dogs continually left around the hospital; they could see that. I told them about the food the dogs ate off patients' plates; they agreed it was a serious problem. I reminded them that killing stray dogs was perfectly legal and that the government was actually ordering that it be done; they knew that.

"As part of your job, then," I said to them, "we must ask you to kill these dogs."

Silence.

"Working in the hospital is a privilege, you know. Along with it you have to expect a few unpleasant duties."

"It's not our custom," said one of the sweepers, a surly young man who generally spoke for his fellows.

"But you kill chickens and goats all the time," I said.

"That's different. It's not our custom to kill dogs."

144

Finally after much discussion, I suggested that if I killed the first dog, maybe they would agree to kill the others. To my surprise, they all jumped at the suggestion. I later discovered they never intended to kill any dogs, but they saw my offer as a way out of the present impasse. They would negotiate killing the next dog another time.

I regretted my offer the moment I spoke, but it was too late to retract it. Deciding I might as well get it over with, I asked Tej to lure the first victim out to the incinerator behind the hospital. Armed with an iron pipe and carrying a scrap of goat meat, I went out intending to dispatch the animal with one stroke. Even though I had chosen an inconspicuous site for the execution, about fifty spectators had already gathered to watch (and by the time I finished, at least fifty more had joined them). I cautiously sneaked up behind the animal, drew my breath, and delivered a mighty blow to its head. But just before the stroke landed, the dog turned slightly, and my blow glanced off its head and onto its shoulder. The animal swung around. Snarling ferociously, it charged at me. I was caught off guard, and the only thing that saved me from being badly bitten was the dog's injured shoulder, which slowed it down just enough for me to get in another blow to its head. The rest is too gruesome to describe. It took twelve more blows to end the misery for both of us.

I was certain that after my demonstration no one in Amp Pipal would ever again kill a dog. But I was wrong; I began offering a bonus for each dog killed, and before long people were demanding bonuses right and left—even for killing dogs that never existed. We put a stop to that hanky-panky by demanding they produce the dog's tail before they got any money.

In the early days, we had to make up administrative policies for the hospital, including rules and regulations for the staff, such as working hours, holidays, salaries, and standards of conduct. What salaries different workers should earn was a particularly thorny question that generally provoked a lively discussion. A sweeper or laundryman received ten dollars a month; an assistant nurse, twenty. The salaries have more than doubled since then, but they are still barely sufficient for living. Even so, our staff members are far better off than most of their neighbors who have no jobs.

As far as possible, our rules of employment made allowance for Hindu customs. For example, whenever a close relative died, a staff member could take up to ten days' emergency leave to perform the necessary funeral rites. This was hard on the doctors because we would suddenly discover that our chief operating-room assistant was gone for the week—or the X-ray technician, or the pharmacist. As the workload gradually increased, we added more staff, but we could never afford to employ enough to cover for these and other unexpected absences. Since the patients ultimately had to pay for our services, we felt obliged to keep their bill as low as possible by not overstaffing the hospital. As it was, staff salaries accounted for almost half of our operating expenses. The old dispensary at Amp Pipal had been much cheaper because it had taken so few people to run it.

Another common cause of unexpected absences was sickness. And maternity leave for the women, although never unexpected, always seemed to come at the worst time as far as staffing requirements were concerned. The frustrations of having to get along without needed staff plagued us continually.

Sita, my office assistant, was such a case. I always dreaded her absences, for I had come to depend on her greatly. She not only helped with individual patients but, more importantly, she kept the outpatient clinic running smoothly. Besides, I have her to thank for keeping me out of a great deal of mischief.

Sita was a member of Sister Mabel's second class, a girl so sweet and demure that initially no one realized how quick-witted she was. She fell in love with a boy in her class and married him—the only legitimate staff love affair I can remember in the history of the Amp Pipal Hospital. (All the others have been illicit.) After her marriage she did not let the male staff push her around as much, especially the Brahmin X-ray technician who used to disparage her mercilessly. He was piqued that a mere female should have earned such respect from the doctors. The males on our staff could never bring themselves to regard women as equals.

Marriage ultimately took its toll on Sita. Her husband went away for more education and left her alone with her *saasu* (mother-in-law), who gave her, according to custom, the most menial chores in the household. She also demanded Sita's monthly pay from the hospital. In addition to working a punishing eight-hour day in the clinic, Sita had to walk an hour to and from work each day.

After two babies, she developed a kidney infection. Time and again she dragged herself to the hospital only to be sent home again, too sick to work. We could never be sure from one day to the next whether she would be helping in the clinic. She was about due with her third baby when one morning she didn't show up at all. The next day we heard she had left for work the previous morning as usual, had delivered her baby alone on the trail, and had taken it back home. Obviously, working mothers in Nepal have special problems, and those problems don't make staffing a hospital any easier.

Staff members are always coming to the nursing superintendent to request time off. We require that they give at least a week's notice to allow the nursing superintendent time to rearrange the duty roster. But in rural Nepal, nothing is planned that far ahead. At one particularly difficult time, when many were already absent due to sickness or holiday, one young assistant nurse went to the nursing superintendent and asked for the next two days off.

"Absolutely not!" the nursing superintendent replied.

"But it's very important."

"Pah, it's always very important. I can't give you the next two days. You should have given me notice. I have no one extra to do your duty."

"But I simply can't come."

"You'll have to." Then, as an afterthought, she asked, "What do you need the time off for?"

"I'm getting married tomorrow."

"Married? Couldn't you have told me before today?"

"I only found out today."

The groom hadn't known much sooner; he had been studying in Kathmandu and had been called home only the previous day. At least the two already knew each other, which is not the case with many couples. Often in Nepal, the bride and groom meet for the first time at the wedding. One thing can be said for these arranged marriages: they save on the heartaches of courtship.

The girl was given two days off.

Sometimes absences are not so legitimate. I once gave my chief operating-room assistant, Buddhi Gurung, a small scholarship to enable him to complete high school and granted him a special five-month study leave. His absence was a great loss to our fledgling surgical program, for we had no one nearly as capable to take his place. Thus I was keenly disappointed when Buddhi didn't return at the end of his five months; he had decided on his own to continue his studies a few months longer.

When he eventually returned, he couldn't understand why I was upset. He felt that the time we had given him simply had not been enough. In the end I forgave him and gave him his job back. Aside from another study leave, which lasted three years, he has remained my chief surgical assistant for most of our time in Amp Pipal. He not only helps me at surgery but also does many of the simpler operations himself. A better assistant I never expect to find anywhere.

During Buddhi's three-year absence, however, I was not so fortunate. His replacement was a rude and cocky young man named Dom Bahadur, who was bright but totally unreliable. During his tenure, he gave us much grief. One thing after another went wrong: Instruments were lost or misplaced, supplies exhausted, equipment was contaminated or roughly handled. And he seemed to care not in the slightest. Hardly any operation went smoothly from beginning to end, and only God's mercy allowed us to escape a succession of tragedies during those years. Yet as a surgical assistant, he exhibited speed and dexterity, which were essential. We decided to keep him since we had no certainty we could find someone better. Often we could not tell for months how a new trainee would turn out. Some were a pleasant surprise; others, a disappointment.

One day Dom Bahadur came to me asking for a loan of one thousand rupees (eighty dollars). We had a revolving loan fund that had been set up to help our staff acquire land or build houses; when Dom said he needed the loan to buy land, I believed him and gave him the money. The next day he left for India. It wasn't the loss of the money I minded so much; it was the loss of his help.

Dom's scheme evidently failed. Several weeks later he came back, asking our forgiveness and promising to repay the loan. In the meantime we had begun to train someone else to do his job. But shortly afterward the new trainee suddenly left, and we were again without help. Rather than gamble on somebody new and have to go through those first painful months of training again, I chose to rehire Dom Bahadur, even over the objections of our missionary nurses, who didn't like him for his impertinence. If I hadn't been the one doing the surgery, I would have shared their feelings completely.

Unhappily, Dom Bahadur had not reformed. We suffered for almost two more years before he left once more without warning—this time to go to Saudi Arabia to plant trees in the desert, for which he was reputedly to get six thousand rupees a month, more than he could earn in a year at Amp Pipal. Thousands of Nepali laborers were being invited to Saudi Arabia to work on reclamation projects, we were told; the government of Nepal was eager to cooperate because it stood to gain a chunk of those salaries in taxes.

Dom never made it to Arabia. In a few months, he returned and asked for his job back. But we'd had enough. He never worked for us again. At about the same time he left, Buddhi returned from his studies and resumed his duties of running the operating room and keeping the surgeon down off the ceiling. There was less wear on the ceiling with Buddhi around.

Staffing problems arise not only among the Nepalis but among the missionaries as well. And missionary staffing problems tend to have fewer solutions. In early years, Helen, Cynthia, and I generally managed to cover for each other. More recently other doctors have been assigned to Amp Pipal and still others have come to relieve us for furloughs or holidays. But even then we have had too few doctors. For the first eight years, for example, we had no one extra to cover our holidays; for our first two furloughs, we could find no fully trained surgeon to take my place. Besides, even doctors get sick and injured. One doctor who was relieving for Helen's furlough slipped on the path and hurt his back; he was out for a month. Helen herself slid off the trail one night and dislocated her elbow. And there have been many other times when one doctor or more has been away, leaving those who remained to continue as best they could.

The periodic lack of crucial help in the business office or in the maintenance department, however, has been as bad as the lack of doctors. At one impossible juncture, we urgently needed a maintenance supervisor, a business manager, and a nursing superintendent all at once. The nursing superintendent we finally found (a British woman), but the other two were not as easy. We eventually recruited a young Christian accountant from South India, Thomas Varughese, to take over as business manager. I spent a fair share of my time helping him at the outset, but he learned the ropes quickly and soon was shouldering most of the business matters himself. Thomas stayed with us two years and did an excellent job. He was followed in rapid succession by Alan Pang from Singapore, Ken Webster, the department store executive from Australia, and lastly Esa Ahonen, a Finnish business administrator. Stu Amstutz of Ohio preceded Thomas. Our outfit was as multinational as anyone could ask for.

As for the desperately needed maintenance supervisor, we could find no one. So the job fell to me—the one who can't even keep a kerosene lamp lit. Our young Nepali maintenance man had some experience, but he was an unpredictable individual with ideas of his own. I wouldn't have minded that he didn't always tell me what he was doing if I could have been sure that he knew himself. But he frequently started something he couldn't handle and then wouldn't admit it. Furthermore he had been dishonest on several occasions and had to be watched, which took more of my time than I could afford to spare. As a result, I was forever being called out of the clinic to see a landslide, to inspect a fallen wall, to okay the purchase of thatch for one of the staff houses, or to deal with some other matter about which I knew little or nothing.

We bumbled along until our maintenance worker announced he had to go to India for eight weeks. As it was a matter of critical importance to him, I couldn't say no. I wrote our mission headquarters in Kathmandu and asked if they could send someone—anyone—to help during his absence. I suggested that perhaps a new missionary language student could come (there were a couple of engineer-builder types in the language school at the time). I promised the job would require no more than an hour a day so he could continue his language study without interruption.

Headquarters came to our rescue for four out of the eight weeks. They sent us a British engineer named Dave Fulford. Dave was glad, I recall, for the chance to get out of Kathmandu into the relaxed atmosphere of Amp Pipal. We were both confident his language study wouldn't suffer in the slightest.

The night he arrived, however, an unusual thing happened: A Nepali house near the hospital caught fire. It belonged to a Christian couple with four children. Although neither parent was home when the blaze started, the four youngsters escaped unharmed. Ordinarily there is no stopping a fire in a thatch-roofed Nepali house because there is seldom enough water at hand. The nearest spring may be fifteen to thirty minutes away. But here the pipe from one of the hospital's two water sources ran underground only a few yards from the house. A quick-thinking neighbor grabbed his spade, dug down to the pipe, and chopped it in two. Presto, water in abundance.

We learned about the fire the next morning at about the same time we discovered the hospital had no water. When we realized the pipe had been cut, David went up to rejoin it. We marveled at the timing of his arrival—just when we needed him. Unfortunately, though, the hospital end of the severed pipe had filled with mud during the night, so not a drop of water would go through. The pipe would have to be completely replaced. The job would have taken two or three days if we'd had a replacement pipe on hand, which we didn't. Who knew how long it would take to get pipe from Kathmandu.

We should have had sufficient water for the hospital from our second source, a completely separate spring that fed into its own system of pipes. Why, then, were all the tanks empty? Finding the answer to that question and correcting the problem took Dave exactly two weeks, working full-time. I don't think he opened his language books once.

We hadn't noticed anything wrong with the second system because our water needs had been adequately met by the first system. With the first system out of commission, we realized the second system had been dry all the time. Somewhere water was leaking out as fast as it ran in. So here we were at the end of the monsoon rains, the land literally dripping, even running with water, but not a drop coming out of the hospital taps.

This problem was actually nothing new. Our pipelines had given us trouble for years. The piping was of poor quality and easily damaged; it was especially vulnerable to rats, who, liking its taste, chewed through it regularly. Often it split apart by itself and leaked underground for days before anyone could locate the defect. We usually tried to find a wet patch of earth to lead us to the leak. But at the end of the monsoons, the earth was wet everywhere, so finding a leak was next to impossible.

Sometimes clogs, not leaks, dried up our taps. A popular

form of vandalism was to dump dirt into the tanks, usually in retaliation for being refused a job at the hospital. And once we discovered four rats in the main tank: two dead, two alive. One of the dead ones was plugging the outlet.

This particular water shortage came at the worst possible time. We were between two very important Hindu festivals, *Dasai* and *Tihar,* always the busiest two weeks of the year. Caring for fifty inpatients a day, one hundred and fifty outpatients, and performing a full schedule of surgery—all without water—was an interesting trick. We quickly hired a few porters to carry water three hundred yards from a spring located slightly below the hospital. They created a kind of water brigade. This temporary arrangement gave us at least enough water to wash the pus and blood off our hands.

For a tiny hospital, the water system was frustratingly complicated—the more so because no one knew exactly where the pipes ran. So David's first task was to locate them. Not knowing the language thwarted his labors, but we had no one who could interpret for him. We assigned a junior maintenance worker to help him, but otherwise David was on his own. For days whenever I met him, he was peering into a freshly dug hole, looking for pipes. It became a joke. After almost two weeks of searching, David finally found the leak, deep under the cement floor of the main hospital corridor. Within hours our tanks were full, and the crisis had passed. David, worn to a frazzle, promptly came down with a severe case of typhoid fever and spent the next two weeks in bed. He returned to Kathmandu looking as if he'd been four years in a prison camp instead of four weeks in the restful village of Amp Pipal.

A few months later, we were sent a full-time maintenance supervisor, a missionary from Manitoba, Canada, and my maintenance headaches came to an end. An entirely new water system was installed using a new kind of heavy leak-proof pipe. We never had a pipe problem again. That is not to say we didn't have periodic water shortages. Water taps were frequently left open somewhere—Nepali villagers weren't any more familiar with taps than with toilets—and if it stayed open all night, the tanks would be empty by morning, especially in the dry season during March through June.

Not long ago our headquarters in Kathmandu decided that our Nepali maintenance man was by this time proficient enough that a missionary maintenance supervisor was no longer necessary. If a situation arose that he couldn't solve, we were to send to Kathmandu for help. Since our maintenance man could handle most things, we were content with the decision. Shortly after our missionary maintenance supervisor left, we began to get a string of poorly developed films, so I called in our X-ray technician to ask what was the matter. He had always turned out films of high quality, even though he had no formal training, so I was not surprised when he said something was wrong with the X-ray machine. I sent for our maintenance man, even though I knew that a malfunction in the X-ray machine was beyond him. As expected, he had no idea what to do. I asked our X-ray technician once more, "Have you checked everything? Are you sure the problem's not something simple that we can fix ourselves?"

"Of course I'm sure," he replied. "It has to be the machine. I've checked everything else." He gave us a look that signified there was no point questioning him further.

So we sent our former project mail carrier (the murderer who, since his release from jail a year earlier, had become our special runner for emergency errands) off to Kathmandu with a letter asking that one of the mission maintenance consultants come and look at our X-ray machine. The Nepali who arrived two days later was indeed a skilled and highly trained electrical technician, but his field of expertise did not include X-ray equipment. He spent a day going over our machine but found nothing. He asked our X-ray technician about his developing solution and about his techniques for exposing films, but our man took offense and responded in such a huffy manner that no further questions were asked.

The nearest X-ray service agency for our machine was in Dacca, Bangladesh, two countries away. To fly a repairman from Dacca to Nepal would be costly, but it had to be done. So again the next morning, the errand runner returned to Kathmandu with a letter asking someone at headquarters to wire the agency in Dacca requesting that a repairman be sent immediately.

One day later the X-ray technician came into my office to show me an X-ray he had just taken. It was perfect! As I looked at him questioningly, I imagined the man in Dacca getting ready to board the plane for Kathmandu.

"What's going on?" I asked sharply.

I had never seen him look abject before, but today he was white with embarrassment.

"I got to thinking," he finally mumbled, "that I had better check my developing solution once more . . ."

Possibly an expletive escaped my lips here, but I quickly suppressed further comment. Obviously the man was deeply ashamed. He knew what it cost to bring the X-ray man from Dacca; the cost to his pride was even greater. And I wasn't feeling all that complacent myself; after all, I'd been signing the letters asking for help.

There was nothing to do but find someone to take another message to headquarters asking them to send a second telegram to Dacca canceling the first one—on the slim chance that it wasn't already too late. Eighteen hours had passed since the first runner left. Finding someone to go to

Kathmandu on a moment's notice was extremely difficult; few had ever been there, and those who had were usually engaged in work of their own and were not free to leave. (This was why our ex-mailman/murderer was so useful: He knew Kathmandu well and, since he was unemployed, he was always available). We eventually found a hospital employee who was willing to go, so I sent him off with my latest letter.

As it happened, no telegram had been sent to Dacca after all. Our mission people had found out that a person familiar with X-ray machines was in Pokhara working with another agency, so they had sent our runner back on the same highway past Dumre to Pokhara, forty miles farther to the west. There he had contacted the X-ray specialist, who agreed to come to Amp Pipal the following day. The first runner returned from Pokhara with this news just a few hours too late; the second runner had already left for Kathmandu. Somehow they had missed each other on the trail.

There was just time enough for the first runner to get back to Pokhara and stop the X-ray specialist before he left the next morning. So after a quick cup of tea, off went the exhausted ex-mailman back down the trail to Dumre, six hours away, and then by bus to Pokhara, three hours away. Both runners arrived back in Amp Pipal the following day at about the same time, their missions accomplished. They undoubtedly wondered what in thunder I thought I was doing sending them on a monkey chase over central Nepal—and for nothing. The second runner brought back a helpful note from headquarters in Kathmandu that read: "We've gone to a lot of trouble to help get you straightened out up there in Amp Pipal. Next time try checking your solutions first."

There wasn't going to be a next time. Our X-ray caper was over.

chapter fourteen

Discipline

YOU CAN OPERATE A HOSPITAL without an X-ray machine, even without water, but you can't operate for long without a staff. Not even an hour.

Our staff members, with few exceptions, are hard-working, conscientious, and amiable. They enjoy their work, along with its salary and prestige. They are not selfish schemers; rather they are community-spirited and as loyal to the hospital as we could ever expect.

Over the years, however, some of their innocence has given way to a rising spirit of nationalism and an increasing desire for affluence. They have discovered that the hospital won't run without them, and they have become more and more ready to use their collective strength to advance their purposes—purposes that may or may not be in the best interest of the patients. As administrators, we are caught between the need to run a safe and efficient hospital and the need to support the legitimate aspirations of our staff. In the early years, it was possible to satisfy both needs simultaneously; in later years, it became increasingly difficult. Our task is made more difficult because we are guests in Nepal, guests who at the same time must exercise authority over Nepali nationals. Being a humble missionary servant under such circumstances is not easy.

I doubt if disciplining wayward national staff was ever part of anyone's missionary vision. But whether they've liked it or not, it has become the responsibility of more than a few missionaries. If we are decisive, consistent, and fair, staff members will generally accept our discipline. If an individual is caught stealing, for example, the staff will ordinarily support our decision to expel the offender, partly because of the disgrace the person brings on his fellow employees. But they leave the catching to us; they will rarely turn in one of their own members. The greater shame is not in the act but in getting caught in the act. If the thief is unknown, the collective disgrace is not as great.

Discipline for negligence is less clear-cut. At what point is a farmboy with a sixth-grade education guilty of negligence? Or an illiterate sweeper? We had a delightful old sweeper named Prem Bahadur who was a natural clown and mimic. He was frequently asked to impersonate departing missionaries or Nepali staff at farewell parties. He was loyal and honest, and loved by all. He had only one defect: He was a terrible sweeper. The presence of dirt, even if he saw it, never seemed to trigger any reaction. He was determinedly slow: I doubt he would have moved any faster if his pants had caught fire. Worse, however, was his recurring abuse of the hospital generator. One of the sweeper's duties was to turn the generator on at sundown and off at bedtime (nine-thirty). At one point we had a small three-kilovolt Japanese generator that was supposed to operate within a certain range clearly demarcated on a little gauge with a bright red pointer. Part of the sweeper's responsibility was to see that the generator remained within this range. But whenever the old fellow was on the evening shift, the red pointer rarely stayed within its prescribed limits. Time and again Prem was reminded and shown, and each time he said, yes, he understood perfectly, and then he'd get it right—as long as we stood there. Finally the reminders turned to reprimands, then to warnings; but nothing affected his performance. We could have relieved him of the evening duty, I suppose, but that wouldn't have been fair to the other sweepers: All were expected to take their turn on the unpopular shifts.

Apparently Prem was incompetent to do even the work of a sweeper. But when word got out that we were considering firing him, the staff rallied to his support. A delegation met with me to discuss the matter. Prem had worked at the hospital three years, they said; he was desperately poor with seven children. We couldn't fire him just because he couldn't keep track of a little red pointer.

"Yes, but he's ruining the generator," I said. "That's no small matter. And we've certainly given him enough chances; this has been going on for months, and he still doesn't do what we say."

"Maybe he can't see," suggested our senior pharmacy technician, an unusually sympathetic, kind-hearted Brahmin lad who was always quick to excuse another's conduct and to defend the downtrodden.

The possibility that the old sweeper couldn't see would have explained a lot of things, but it didn't explain why he could see the pointer perfectly well when we showed it to him.

When I pointed this out to the pharmacist, he asked, "When you talk to Prem about this, it's always the next day, isn't it? Maybe he has trouble seeing at night. Why don't you try giving him some vitamin A?"

Vitamin A deficiency—night blindness. Of course! And indeed, that's what was troubling the old sweeper. A little vitamin A and his problem with the pointer was solved. Listening to our staff was always worthwhile. This wasn't the first time they kept me out of the spinach. And it wouldn't be the last.

Pashupatinath, the most revered Hindu shrine in Nepal, is a temple dedicated to Shiva. Along the river bank are apartments for those with terminal illnesses who have been brought by relatives to die near the river, as is the Hindu custom.

The firewood has arrived. An important reason families hasten to move dying relatives to the river is their fear that the soul, if it cannot immediately find access to the river, will escape the body and wander about to haunt surviving family members.

The castle of Prithwi Narayan Shah, who united Nepal in the mid-1700s, is Nepal's "Mount Vernon." The village of Amp Pipal straddles the distant ridge to the left while the 26,000-foot Annapurna Range rises in the background.

The Amp Pipal Hospital as viewed from Liglig mountain. The author's home is the farthest house to the right. Ridge after ridge lead up to 25,800-foot Himalchuli, eighteen miles away. Trails, such as those seen in the center, are the arteries of commerce and communication, since the sole means of transportation is by foot. The terrain is rough for the healthy; it is even more difficult for the sick, who, on the average, must trek a day's journey to reach the hospital.

The Amp Pital Hospital as seen from the author's front yard. The Chepe River lies 2,000 feet below; in the distance the Annapurna Range rises 26,000 feet.

The forty-bed Amp Pipal Hospital is surrounded by terraced fields. The skyline is dominated by Himalchuli, which rises 25,800 feet.

The *ping*, or Himalayan ferris wheel, is operated by foot but attains great speed, and its free-swinging seats often clobber bystanders. The *ping* is one of the most common causes of injury in rural Nepal, equivalent to the automobile in developed countries.

This is the view from just above the author's house, looking toward the Annapurna Range.

A typical Nepali house made of mud and stone.

One of Nepal's greatest needs is clean and abundant drinking water. Here water has been piped into a village from a distant, year-round source. In most villages, women must walk up to an hour to fetch the family's needs for the day. With only one jug of water per family per day, the Western ideal of cleanliness is as unattainable for average Nepalis as it is incompatible with their thinking.

The *diki,* or rice husker, is foot operated, calling to mind the virtual absence of machinery in rural Nepal. The girl on the left must be quick as she gathers the rice, lest her fingers get crushed by the falling beam.

The oil press is used to extract oil from mustard seed or syrup from sugar cane. Underlying these quaint and tranquil scenes of domestic activity is the unmitigated drudgery of Nepal's women.

Farming in the Himalayan foothills. Ninety-five percent of Nepal's people earn their living from the land.

This is "Main Street" in Amp Pipal. A wedding procession, made up of the friends and family of the groom, is on its way to fetch the bride three hours away. A Family Planning sign on the far right is an appropriate, if unwelcome, reminder at wedding time.

Ninety percent of Nepal's people would be judged poor by any standard. This mother with her two sons typifies the approaching crisis faced by most of Nepal's families. According to Nepali custom, a family's land is divided equally between the sons. In the case of this family, whose land is even now insufficient, what future lies in store for these two boys?

A middle-class couple. This young man exhibits all four signs of the middle class in Nepal: dark glasses, umbrella, shoes, and, above all, a transistor radio.

The young girl in the bridal box is leaving home for the first time to be married to a man she has never met. Divorce in Nepal is uncommon because a woman is rarely able to divorce her husband, and the husband, if he tires of his first wife, doesn't divorce her. He keeps her to work in his fields and he finds a new wife, even though a government law forbids polygamy.

A young man carries his mother home from the hospital following surgery. She has recovered, but is still too weak to walk the day's journey over a mountain to her home.

Ambulance. This man is on his way to the hospital.

Moving van. The most unusual item to be carried up the mountain to Amp Pipal was Cynthia's piano. It took thirteen men two days to accomplish the task. Cynthia played them a piece when they arrived, but they were unimpressed.

Taxi. It is not only patients who are carried in baskets—it may be your mother-in-law. Cynthia's mother, having arrived for a visit, starts up the mountain to Amp Pipal.

The author's house and garden shortly after his arrival in Amp Pipal.

If one is invited out and forgets to bring utensils, none will be provided, as Cynthia found out on this occasion. The absence of a spoon is no deterrent to Christopher, however, who is enjoying the meal immensely. Notice Nepal's version of the paper plate.

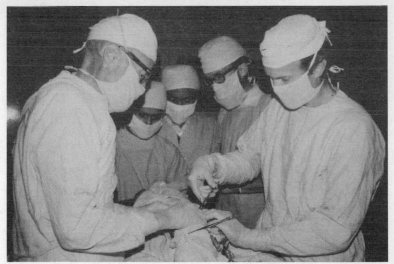

The author is assisted at surgery by his father, Dr. Thomas Hale, Sr., who was a practicing surgeon before entering hospital administration. (Photo by Dr. Cynthia Hale.)

An important aspect of medical work in developing countries is training national paramedical workers. This is the first assistant nurse class at the Amp Pipal Hospital. On the left is Mabel McLean, of Scotland, hospital nursing supervisor.

The doorway of the clinic is crowded with village women waiting to be examined. Most have never seen a doctor and are apprehensively watching his every move, wondering what *their* turn will be like.

Further north the communities become more isolated, and the inhabitants less familiar with Westerners and their gadgets, which often provoke much wonder and curiosity.

(Right) The tooth is out; the doctor is happy. The patient is less so. (Below) Friendship is restored with the usual Nepali sign of greeting. She'll feel better tomorrow. (Photos by Dicran Berberian.)

Where there is no bridge, travelers have the indescribable delight of crossing on a *twing,* a wonderful name because it aptly describes the sensation felt in your heart halfway across. The author has crossed on this *twing* a number of times on his way to Barpak.

The population of Barpak has outstripped its means of support, so the residents terrace slopes so steeply (left) that the vertical part is up to ten feet high while the horizontal part is only three feet wide. We are no longer surprised to hear Nepalis tell of "falling out of their fields."

Cynthia, Tommy, and Christopher, shortly after our arrival in Nepal in 1970.

Author with (left to right) Amrit, Prakash, Jiwan, and Megh Nath. (Photo by Asbjorn Voreland.)

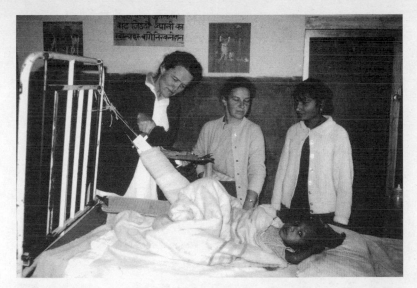

Dr. Helen Huston making rounds.

Tej, the hospital laundryman, doing his monkey dance at the author's home while other staff members watch approvingly.

Krishna, the orphan from whom the author removed a bladder stone as big as a baseball.

Shaktaman Ghale and his mother on a return visit to the hospital.

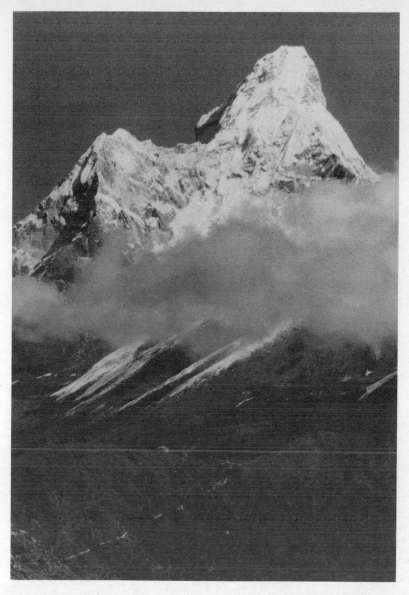

Ama Dablan, 22,494 feet, towers above the Tengboche monastery in the center foreground.

The summit of Everest appears at the left. Lhotse, at 27,890 feet, is seen in the clouds at the center, and Ama Dablan, at 22,494 feet, rises on the right. Tengboche monastery is seen in the center foreground.

Discipline for sexual misconduct was an even thornier matter. For the first time in this rural society, young men and women were thrown together in a common working situation that allowed unprecedented opportunity for forming alliances. One after another of our staff succumbed to the attractions of the opposite sex. Fortunately for us, the scruples of Nepali Hindu society were almost as sensitive as our own, and our standards of conduct were generally upheld by the community.

Our missionary women were particularly scandalized by the behavior of some of our young people; they were also the last to know what was happening. The entire village would know someone was pregnant months before any of the missionaries would find out about it. Naturally we made every effort to keep track of our girls and protect them from the designs of unscrupulous men. For example, we kept strict watch on the nurses' residence, and any male who ventured to enter courted instant dismissal. Neither were girls allowed in the male residences. But, of course, there were many ways to get around such strictures. Tej provided one way: The upper floor of the mission house where he lived was a favorite trysting place for many couples until we discovered it and made him move. Tej claimed ignorance, which could have been true since he was often high on drugs. But even if Tej's house was not available, there were plenty of other places, including the jungle in the warm season.

Only once was anyone caught in the act—at the hospital of all places—during our second year in Amp Pipal. Two infants were born one winter day, and since the hospital isn't heated, they were placed in homemade hot-water bottle "incubators" and moved to the nursing station where the assistant nurse could keep an eye on them. Early in the evening, the night sweeper, an old man named Giri, found them screaming full blast with no nurse in sight. Taking care of newborn babies was not part of his job, but the screaming got on his nerves so he decided to take them to their mothers so they could get something to eat. But he couldn't tell whose baby was whose, and being unable to read, he searched for the nurse. The nurse on duty that night was a recent graduate of Sister Mabel's first assistant nurse course, a pretty young girl who had proved to be both conscientious and able. But tonight she was nowhere to be found.

After looking in all the usual places, Giri finally found her in a vacant private room—in bed with a young man. Amazed and embarrassed, Giri slammed the door shut and called to the nurse that her babies were screaming. The young man, meanwhile, jumped out the window and escaped into the night. Giri could not see who he was.

Giri, a man of strong principles, was offended by the nurse's behavior. So first thing the next morning, he reported the matter to Dr. Helen and Sister Mabel. The news, I must say, electrified the two women. If they had any foreboding of what was happening among some of our staff, this clinched it: The hospital was turning into a house of immorality.

The girl was immediately dismissed, which brought the predictable repercussions. The very next night the girl's family and friends, together with some neighborhood hotheads, gathered at Giri's house near the hospital and tried to intimidate the sweeper into changing his story. They assumed the girl was innocent, that Giri was a liar, and that the hospital administration had acted unjustly. The girl, who was also there, denied all wrongdoing. Some of them threatened to beat Giri, and if that failed to change things, they were prepared to "tear down the hospital." Things got so hot that Giri finally went up and roused Helen and Mabel from their beds to come down and face the angry group themselves and explain why they had dismissed the girl. It was 2 A.M.

Giri not only stood firm but persuaded most of those present that his story was true. Finally the girl herself broke down and admitted her transgression. This, of course, changed everything: The hapless nurse then became the recipient of the group's wrath. She had disgraced and humiliated her family and had violated the moral code of the community. Her father demanded to know who the young man was. If he was of the right caste, she would be forced to marry him. If not, she would be thrown out of her home and village and left to beg for her living. She would be unfit to marry anyone else.

When she finally gave the name of the young man, everyone reacted with shock and disbelief. He was the brother of our Christian pharmacist, a woman of Nepali extraction whose family came from Darjeeling, India. He was a shiftless fellow who had come to visit his sister three months before. He had been seen frequently at the hospital in the evenings, and on several occasions Mabel had asked him to leave. His conduct with various nurses had been so loose that only the day before we had told him that he could no longer stay in the project. This had upset his sister the pharmacist, who promptly announced that if her brother were sent away, she would leave too, and if she went, so would her husband who happened to be our assistant business manager. We were in a difficult situation. She was the only pharmacist we had, and the husband was just as badly needed in the business office. But this was all before the 2 A.M. meeting. Now that the brother's guilt had been established, it would be easier to get rid of him—the Nepalis would see to it.

The worst part of the matter for us was that the young man had been posing as a member of the local church and was regarded as a Christian by all the villagers. Now we'd be held in contempt all the more—a trifling minority in a hostile land, already suspect, now discredited. A Christian boy violating a Hindu girl in a Christian hospital! What a sensation it created at Giri's house that night. They were all popping like corn in the pan, Mabel and Helen right along with the villagers. It was a dark moment in the history of our project.

It was even darker for the girl. With both the villagers and her own family berating her mercilessly, she finally realized how great her crime had been. Her lover was not just low caste, he was *no* caste—an outcast Christian and a foreigner, an Indian. She had defiled herself, and in so doing had ostracized herself forever from her family and her village. She broke down in tears of remorse and despair.

Early the next morning, the pharmacist, her husband, and the brother left the project, no doubt fearing the vengeance of the community. The assistant nurse was eventually sheltered by one of her brothers. Some years later she married a fine young man and has since been happily raising a family—in defiance of the curse placed on her that night by the village elders. The younger generation's relaxed view of marriage, although not altogether commendable, at least gives young people the chance to start again.

One hero emerged from the sordid affair: Giri. All agreed he had acted courageously and honorably. He had shown himself to be a master of group psychology. He was not a Christian as far as we knew but he had a remarkable ability to quote from the Bible, a talent he had used effectively the night of the meeting. He had astounded everyone, especially Sister Mabel, who was not easily astounded. Thanks mostly to Giri, the episode blew over quickly.

We were not always so fortunate. Disciplining most affairs of the flesh generated much acrimony and gave us hassles and headaches for weeks. Even the missionaries didn't always agree. Matching the punishment to the offense was always the biggest problem. In any given case, some would call for a harsh penalty, while others would favor a mild one or none at all. No two cases were exactly alike, so the debate was renewed each time. The community at large, in addition to our staff, freely took sides (sometimes demanding punishment where we thought none was indicated). No matter what decision we made, we could be sure some would vociferously oppose it.

Our greatest wrath was usually reserved for married male staff members who compromised the single girls under our care; on this, both Nepalis and Westerners agreed. And yet it wasn't always fair to blame just the boys. We once had two sisters on our staff, Busang and Bumang, who were Sherpas, a tribe not noted for the chastity of its women. Within a short time, they managed to ensnare two of our young married men, a Brahmin and a *Chetri* (the warrior caste). It was futile, of course, to try to determine who had seduced whom, though some tried anyway: The boys had been willing partners, and that was enough. According to the rules of the mission and the mores of the community, we had little choice but to fire all four. They paid for their pleasure with their jobs.

The day after they were fired, the Brahmin's father, along with ten friends and relatives, came to our house to plead with me for his son's job. When that failed, the young man himself came the following day, bringing with him both his old wife and his new Sherpa bride, the new wife carrying the two-month-old baby of the older one.

To my amazement, the first wife did most of the talking. She begged me to forgive her husband and to approve his new marriage. Their own marriage, she said, had been arranged without his consent when they were very young and should no longer be binding on him. She also promised to help raise any children the new marriage might produce, so that the new wife could continue to work at the hospital. I detected no sign that she had been coerced to say this; she spoke naturally and earnestly.

The husband then pledged to care for his first wife and their two children as he had always done—a major concession since most first wives were left pretty much to shift for themselves. I wavered. While they were still there, the pradhan panch and several schoolteachers arrived to argue on behalf of the husband, whose family, I was discovering, was quite influential in the community. According to the pradhan panch, the worst they had done was to marry outside their caste. Especially for a Brahmin, to marry a noncaste tribeswoman was extremely unbefitting, even in modern Nepal. For the new wife, it had been a downward step, too. Sherpas considered themselves to be the highest caste of all, with the Brahmins a poor second.

Our dilemma was sharpened by our fondness for the Sherpa girls. They were excellent workers, cheerful and tireless. But where I might have wavered, our women missionaries did not. For them the issue was beyond discussion, and the consequences of splitting up our team over the matter were too serious to justify debating it further. So the two couples left. And for weeks afterward, their embittered families and friends harrassed and threatened us and carried out acts of vandalism against the hospital. Nobody won.

We never took sexual sins lightly in Amp Pipal, and we were slow to forgive them. Once a man had two wives we acted as if he had consigned himself permanently to a state of sin from which he could not be restored. Yet once the sin itself had been committed, what was he to do? To shed one of his wives would have been an even greater sin. Was there to be no forgiveness? We weren't so hard on other sins, perhaps even more harmful because of the scant attention we paid them, especially when they occurred in ourselves: intolerance, judgment, anger, irritability, gossip, backbiting. What message had we given these two couples, their families, the community? How could we maintain God's standards without playing the Pharisee? It took more humility than any of us, within ourselves, possessed.

chapter fifteen

Demonstrations and Strikes

O*UR FIRST STRIKE* took place in the hospital's fourth year and lasted half an hour. At the time we had a Finnish nursing superintendent named Sarika. (Her immediate predecessor had been a Swiss missionary, and before her we'd had Sister Mabel.) In temperament, Sarika was as different from Mabel as it was possible to be. Whereas Mabel was solid, even imposing in appearance, and determined in manner, Sarika was petite and airy, with a briskness about her that suggested great activity yet failed to conceal an underlying indecisiveness. The staff sensed at once that she could be bullied, so they challenged her authority in little ways. Consequently Sarika rarely made a decision, even in minor matters, without first being assured of my support. So I was completely surprised one afternoon when some of the staff came to me and announced they would not return to work until one of their members had been exonerated and given back his job.

"What do you mean, 'given back his job'?" I asked. "Has somebody lost his job? What's happened?"

"He's been fired by the nursing superintendent."

"Fired!" That was unbelievable. The decision to fire someone was rarely made, and certainly never alone or quickly but only after much agonizing and prayer. "Who's been fired?"

It was Padam Raj, a young Brahmin lad in Sarika's assistant nurse training class. He was one of six applicants (out of more than sixty) who had been chosen by Sarika herself, with my concurrence, for a place in the class. The trainees were about to graduate and become assistant nurses, but Sarika had accidentally discovered an irregularity in Padam's original application form. He claimed to have passed only seventh grade, whereas in fact he had passed eighth. The class was only open to those *below* eighth grade, so Padam had falsified his application. I can't remember what had aroused Sarika's suspicions, but the thought that one of her own students had deceived her in this manner upset her so violently that she dismissed Padam on the spot.

The staff reacted even more violently. Almost at once the male members accosted Sarika outside her office and began to abuse her verbally. She got angry with them, which didn't help. As they crowded around her, the X-ray technician, a relative of Padam's from the same village, began to push Sarika and even to punch her. Others looked as if they might do the same. Sarika managed to escape back into her office and lock the door, whereupon the staff had stormed up the corridor to my office to inform me they were going on strike.

Sarika obviously had acted precipitously, and in the few seconds I had to think about it, I could hardly agree with her decision. Padam had behaved well and studied hard for an entire year, and had been the most mature and serious-minded student in the class. But I suppressed my initial reaction and merely said I would not overrule the nursing superintendent's decision and that we could talk things over just as well without a strike. I also told them they would not be paid if they went on strike. This was a new thought for them, and it took most of the steam out of their protest.

In view of the nastiness of the attack on Sarika, it seemed

best to stick with her decision, like it or not, and make it clear to the staff that such behavior would accomplish nothing. So we expelled Padam for six months. Some years later he became a Christian and subsequently developed into one of the steadiest members of the local church. Sarika, on the other hand, went home on furlough within a few months of the strike and never returned.

For the next three years, we had no major labor troubles. Then while walking to work one Sunday morning (on what would turn out to be the busiest day we had ever had), I observed, to my surprise, the entire staff grouped together outside the hospital entrance hastily signing a long document. It was a strike ultimatum. They were demanding that I fire Tony, our British laboratory technician. To back up their demand, they were refusing to work until I did so.

I had been only slightly forewarned that trouble was brewing for Tony. He had come to take over the laboratory after our Indian lab technician left in a fright over the unpleasantness that erupted at the time of Nirmala's thievery. In the few years he'd been with us, Tony had dramatically upgraded the laboratory, standardized all the procedures, and trained two Nepalis to run the lab in his place. Then he reorganized the pharmacy, and after that he helped streamline our supply system. Recently I had made him my administrative assistant. His help was invaluable, and both the nursing superintendent and I relied on him for much of the day-to-day administration of the hospital.

Tony was not a regular missionary, that is, he was not supported by churches at home. He was a special employee who drew his salary from a private fund we had set up for such purposes. What kept him so many years in the little village of Amp Pipal working for one tenth the salary he could have gotten in Britain was simply his deep and genuine love for these Nepali hill people. He lived alone on the ridge, half an hour above the hospital, in a Nepali-style house. He knew the language fluently and during his spare time, he often sat for hours in teashops talking with staff and villagers; on evenings and weekends he tutored schoolchildren in English and math. He gave a large share of his meager income to help poor families and to pay the tuition and buy books for needy students. He was close to the people, one with them. Although he never claimed to be a Christian or even religious, he was in many ways a better missionary than the rest of us. And the Nepalis, especially our staff, loved him and confided in him—that is, until he became my administrative assistant.

Suddenly Tony was no longer "one of the boys." He was over them. He was responsible for finding ways to make the hospital run more efficiently, which meant encouraging the staff to work more efficiently. I believe he did it with the utmost tact; he was an English gentleman first and last. But several staff members took offense. Exhibiting the exaggerated hurt so commonly seen in those who are wrong, they attacked Tony and stirred up the rest of the staff against him. Chief among them was old Laxmi, the cleaning lady. Under Sister Mabel's supervision, Laxmi had at least gone through the motions of attending to duty, but under Sarika and later nursing superintendents, she had become slovenly and unmanageable. She regarded the entire hospital as her private smoking parlor and generally could be found in the place farthest removed from any work to be done. She was also a gossip with few equals, a calling she pursued zealously on duty and off.

Laxmi had begun to exasperate her sixth nursing superintendent, a new girl who had been in the country just over a year and who was having so much trouble speaking the language that she was incapable of supervising sixty Nepalis.

171

Apparently the new nursing superintendent had tried to reprimand Laxmi for something. When Laxmi did not understand the reprimand, Tony was called to interpret. Tony dutifully translated the message that if Laxmi's work did not improve she would lose her job. Whereupon old Laxmi promptly spread the word that Tony was going to fire her. So now the staff was rallying to Laxmi's support, eager to avenge this ill-use of their countrywoman at the hands of a foreigner.

Two other trumped-up charges had also been made against Tony, but he was in no way to blame for either of them. One of the alleged offenses had not involved Tony at all but had resulted from a misunderstanding between our new nursing superintendent and our Indian business manager, who also had arrived recently. Some of the staff saw Tony as the cause of their accumulated frustrations and grievances. Taking it out on Tony, their old buddy, was easier than confronting me.

Any day in a hospital is a bad day for a strike, but this one couldn't have been worse. The line of patients waiting to register already extended outside the hospital gate. I met with the staff in the X-ray room. After five minutes of discussion, I realized that only three or four individuals had instigated the strike, each of whom had a personal grudge against Tony. Foremost among them was the X-ray technician. The rest of the staff was against the strike but had succumbed to the wishes of the vocal few. When the staff members realized the charges were groundless, they went back to work, agreeing even to work through their lunch hour to help see all the patients. Although the troublemakers had been discredited, the damage was done. Tony quit the hospital a few months later, discouraged and disillusioned. He didn't leave Nepal, however; he became a teacher in the new Amp Pipal high school, a position he filled fruitfully for an additional three years before finally returning to Britain. His contribution to the people of Amp Pipal will not be soon forgotten.

About this same time we began to detect the first faint signs of a growing restlessness among the young people of Nepal. Even though we were out in the backlands, we began hearing reports of increasing political activity among students around the country, including our own district. Communist youth groups were forming, and other groups opposed to the king were organizing and recruiting supporters. Rumors reached us of clandestine late-night meetings where plans to undermine the panchayat system and destabilize the government were discussed. Even our hospital was the site of several such gatherings, though as soon as we learned of them, we strictly forbade further political meetings on the premises. We were in Nepal at the invitation of the government, and we were not about to take part in any revolutionary activities.

But because we refused to allow such activities, we became a target for the agitators, especially the more radical Communists. We were considered pro-government and anti-Communist. We also learned that our district had one of the strongest Communist party organizations anywhere in the country.

There was, of course, no way we could prevent our staff from taking sides. What they did off the hospital property on their own time was none of our business. Still we were saddened to see them divide into factions, for it meant the loss of the family spirit that had prevailed in the hospital since its beginning. As the political atmosphere heated up, the divisions among our staff became more and more pronounced. Four groups evolved: the Communists, the supporters of the panchayat system, the supporters of the party system, and the Christians, who were opposed by everyone.

The Communists posed the greatest threat to the hospital and to the government. Their avowed intention was to tear down the existing structures and then rebuild them after their own fashion. In pursuit of this goal, they carried out sporadic acts of violence, disrupted established institutions through strikes and demonstrations, and slandered and harrassed anyone who stood in their way. Several members of our staff who led factions opposed to the Communists had been singled out for special persecution. They were in constant danger of being ambushed and physically beaten as they walked home from work.

The king and his ministers attempted to stem the rising opposition as best they could. Since it was by no means clear who would come out on top in the event of a showdown, they wisely refrained from repressive tactics. The government of Thailand recently had been toppled by students; it could happen in Nepal, too.

Unfortunately the students in Nepal responded to the government's moderation by increasing their disruptive activities, mainly in the form of strikes and protest marches. As a result, Nepal entered a prolonged period of instability. At times it was uncertain if the government would be able to maintain order. In our district, for example, students openly flouted their teachers, the pradhan panch, even the police.

Several high school teachers from Amp Pipal were beaten up by their own pupils, and once our pradhan panch was badly roughed up by a group of teenagers. He never showed any heart for cracking down on unruly students after that but went to great lengths to avoid confrontation, often going away on "urgent business" whenever trouble was brewing. He wasn't going to be much help, we could see.

One particularly unpleasant incident took place in Thadipokhari, just down the mountain from Amp Pipal, where Nepal's recently retired prime minister had come to give a speech. Several hundred angry, club-wielding protestors prevented him from speaking, publicly humiliated him, and drove him out of town. The police had been either unable or unwilling to control the rioters. It was an impressive show of strength for the Communists.

During this time we were having our own problems. Two or three of our most influential staff leaders were members of the Communist party and had close links with the Communist-led student unions of several high schools in our part of the district. So whenever an issue arose at the hospital about which they felt strongly, they could quickly call together a mob of students to pressure the rest of the staff into going on strike or forcing us to close the hospital to protect patients and property. They rarely had to use such a show of force, however. Rumors and threats were usually sufficient to intimidate our staff, as well as much of the countryside.

The first real trouble took place one night in 1979, when I was away. Someone tried to break through the mud and stone wall of our hospital business office. For some reason, our night sweeper, whose duties also included being night watchman, never reported the incident. It was inconceivable that he had not heard the noise. He had either been asleep or had been somewhere he shouldn't have been—or he had been in cahoots with the robber.

We had carefully instructed all our sweepers to "look around" the hospital every fifteen to twenty minutes during the night shift to reduce the chances of theft. Furthermore we had warned them they would be held accountable for whatever occurred during their duty hours. A string of blatant robberies had plagued us during the preceding year—five mattresses, forty blankets, and all three microscopes from the laboratory—and it seemed that the only way to make the sweepers take their job seriously was to penalize them for losses that occurred on their shift, a variation of the old practice of executing the jailor if the prisoner escaped.

So the next morning when the broken wall of the business office was discovered, the night sweeper was summoned, and when he could give no satisfactory explanation for his failure to report the break-in, he was fired.

The Communists on the hospital staff saw this as an opportunity to flex their muscle. They persuaded the rest of the staff to strike and then summoned students from Amp Pipal to compel us to give the sweeper back his job. Fortunately for us the former prime minister was due to arrive at Thadipokhari that day, so all the students had gone to join the demonstration against him.

Also on that same day, one of our United Mission executives arrived unexpectedly. He had passed through Thadipokhari at the height of the disturbance against the prime minister and saw firsthand the ugly mood of the rioters. He had just come from Tansen, where recently one of our mission hospitals had been locked in a bitter confrontation with Communists and other agitators, resulting in a ten-day strike. He had not expected to find our staff on strike, too.

In any event, with the arrival of the mission executive, administrative expediency won over firmness and consistency, and the sweeper was reinstated, thus ending our walkout the same day. Of course it didn't end our troubles; if anything, it made them worse. Local strike instigators, emboldened by their success, were determined to press their advantage.

The Communists' primary objective concerning the hospital was to discredit the mission and, in particular, the Nepali Christians on our staff. They began by circulating false and damaging reports about the way we operated the hospital, the exorbitant fees we charged, and the "profits" we skimmed off the backs of poor villagers, which went directly into our pockets. Everything that went wrong, and many things that didn't, were embellished and widely reported. All deaths became proof of our negligence; all treatment failures were evidence of our incompetence.

The Nepali Christians received the greater share of the trouble. Untrue and malicious rumors about their characters and personal lives spread throughout the community. They were threatened with beatings, and their names were given to the police because it was against the law for a Nepali to be a Christian.

Even Nepalis on the staff who might otherwise have remained neutral began to side against them. I'm sure to many Christians it looked as if the mission's days were numbered and that they would be left without a job or even the hope of getting one. Who else would employ them? Their certificates from the hospital's assistant nurse course were not recognized by the government. Many of them didn't even have a certificate.

By the spring of 1980, the situation had become intolerable. The government decided that the best way to defuse the crisis was to hold a national referendum and let the people decide what form of government they wanted: the "party" system or the panchayat system. This was a bold and unprecedented step. The Communist system was not included among the choices; as a result, the Communists and their allies determined to sabotage the referendum and, if possible, prevent it from taking place. So during the months before the voting, the public disturbances increased in frequency and intensity.

Our own difficulties increased as well. Almost daily, small bands of students came to the hospital and hung around or wandered through the wards or outpatient department looking for trouble. We got to know the ringleaders well. Often they would ask to be examined for fictitious ailments and then not have money to pay for the examination.

At the same time, reports filtered in that a large group of students was planning to break hospital windows, wreck the generator, rob the business office, or "get" one or more of the Christians. No one knew whether the reports originated with friends who wanted to warn us or with enemies who wanted to frighten us. However, when the reports did not immediately come true, we began to give them less and less credence and went about our business as if nothing were the matter.

The first serious incident came without warning. One afternoon I was called from the clinic to meet a delegation of fifty students who had stationed themselves outside the hospital business office. They were accusing our purchasing officer, a young Nepali Christian, of cheating some porters out of their wages. The charge had been fabricated with the help of our Communist bookkeeper, an affable man with a ready smile whom we had hired on the recommendation of another mission project where he had worked. We had all come to regret the decision because he was our chief troublemaker and one of the leading Communist organizers in the district. Furthermore he had access to all the books, so when he said anything about the hospital's financial transactions, people assumed he knew what he was talking about. Indeed he did, though he altered the facts to suit his purposes.

Together with the purchasing officer and a few of our hospital staff, I went with the students to the hospital entrance, where still other students had congregated in the meantime. There we spent two hours attempting to reason with a crowd that soon swelled to over two hundred shouting, pushing young people. They demanded that the guilty purchasing officer be handed over to them. When we refused, they grew still angrier and began to press in as if to seize him by force. Indeed they would have, had not our burly Canadian maintenance supervisor and Ken Webster, the business manager, enclosed him in their arms. For an unknown reason, the students were reluctant to attack the foreigners outright, and the purchasing officer was saved from being beaten, quite possibly to death, by the incensed mob. Had they chosen to do so, the crowd could have run over all of us, and we would have been powerless to stop them.

We got a taste that day of what it is like to be on the receiving end of a violent demonstration, to face a mob that is essentially out of control—certainly out of our control. The unsettling experience ended only as night began to fall. Even angry demonstrators had to get home before dark to avoid the spirits. The purchasing officer emerged shaken but unscathed; in fact, he had only been touched once, when the twelve-year-old son of a Christian family living nearby smeared his face with buffalo dung. It was the saddest moment of a sad day.

The next major incident happened about two months later. The nationwide referendum had been held, and the king's panchayat system had won over the party system—2.4 million to 2 million. Close but decisive. The Communists claimed the elections had been rigged, and rumors circulated that they were about to launch a full-scale revolution. It seemed for a time as if the referendum hadn't solved anything.

Then early one Thursday in May, we received several independent reports that a large number of students and other agitators would arrive that same afternoon to "destroy" the hospital and to "deal with" the missionaries and the Nepali Christians on the staff. These reports seemed more serious than others we had received, so we decided that Ken Webster should go down to the local police post in Thadipokhari, two hours down the mountain, and report this new threat to the inspector and ask him to send two or three policemen to the hospital immediately. Then Ken was to go directly to Gorkha, the district capital six hours to the east, and speak with the

Chief District Officer about the need for more permanent police protection in Amp Pipal. I wrote a letter requesting that police be posted at least temporarily in Amp Pipal, that there was considerable antigovernment activity in our vicinity, and that hospital property, personnel, and patients were in jeopardy. I further stated it did us no good to have police stationed two hours away in Thadipokhari. By the time we notified them and they got up the mountain, the damage already would be done.

We had the usual day's work ahead of us, so after Ken left, we began seeing patients in order to get as much done as possible before the excitement began. But by midmorning new rumors indicated that the attack on the hospital had been postponed a day, that we could expect trouble Friday instead.

Exactly four hours after Ken left, three policemen arrived from Thadipokhari. Seeing that everything was peaceful and quiet, they concluded that the rumors were baseless, perhaps the work of a few malcontents, and that we foreigners were needlessly anxious. They questioned a few people, took down names of some radical students, and then, to our surprise and dismay, said they were returning to Thadipokhari. We protested. They were taking the rumors too lightly, we argued. Wouldn't they at least spend the night—at our expense, of course. To our relief, they agreed.

The next day, after eating their morning rice meal, the police were once more ready to leave. But just then a small group of students came down the path toward the hospital. For once I was happy to see them. Now the police might believe us. Several more groups of students followed. Then our pradhan panch appeared, looking not at all his usual suave and confident self. Drawing me aside, he whispered that scores of students from the Amp Pipal high school were on the trail heading for the hospital. He asked me to do my best to get the police to stay. He was too embarrassed to ask himself, since it might suggest he was afraid of the students—which no doubt he was, having already been beaten up once.

The police, fortunately, needed no convincing. They took up positions near the hospital entrance. Soon the main body of students came into view, trooping down the trail from Amp Pipal and to the front of the hospital. But as soon as the students caught sight of the police, they seemed confused and uncertain what to do. They were obviously chagrined that we had been tipped off to their plans, though they did their best not to show it. They stood around for a while, forming little clusters and looking sullen. Then, as if they had merely been out for a stroll, they dispersed quietly along the several trails leading from the hospital.

That evening, through our network of sources, we learned that the students were infuriated that the police had been called and were planning to stage a giant demonstration on Sunday, which is a regular working day in Nepal. Students from all the surrounding high schools would be called to participate. They particularly intended to punish those on our staff who they thought had informed on them. The three policemen kindly agreed to stay until Sunday.

On Saturday Ken returned from Gorkha with word that the Chief District Officer didn't have any spare policemen to station in Amp Pipal. He had enough trouble staffing existing posts. He was sorry, but we would have to send word to Thadipokhari whenever we needed help. At least we would have help through Sunday, which was some consolation.

Sunday morning came. There was little we could do to brace ourselves for the expected disturbance with only three unarmed policemen to protect us and half our staff secretly and not-so-secretly rooting for the students. The day's main event had been billed as a "demonstration," but there was no telling what it might become. They probably called it a demonstration so the police would not be alarmed and call for reinforcements. We knew that the more radical students would not be content with a protest march, but we didn't know if they would succeed in stirring up the crowd to violence. We debated calling for reinforcements before trouble started—after all, they wouldn't arrive until four hours after we called them. But the three policemen thought such a move would be provocative and would only lead to greater trouble. They evidently believed the students were as good as their word, and that if they had scheduled a demonstration, a demonstration was all it would be. The policemen were young, barely older than the students themselves, and if they wanted to take a sanguine view of the situation, we could hardly blame them. They planned to remain on the sidelines and keep out of trouble.

By 8 A.M., the usual crowd of patients had begun lining up to register. Leaving the policemen to wait for the students, we started getting as much of our work done as possible. It was a usual busy Sunday. Several days earlier I had scheduled a kidney stone operation for that morning and I didn't feel I should cancel it. Besides, I thought I could get it done before the students showed up.

I was delayed by some other work, so the operation started late. I was forty minutes into the surgery and had just located the stone in the kidney when Ken Webster, flushed and out of breath, appeared at the door.

"They're coming, hundreds of them," he said. "You can see them on the trail above the hospital. Wherever the trail is in the open, you see students. The line must be half a mile long; it looks like the whole hillside is moving."

Even allowing for hyperbole, the picture was vivid enough. But with my patient's kidney open in front of me, there wasn't much I could do about the situation. We decided to close the hospital temporarily, to send all the outpatients outside, and to lock the doors and shut the gates. No sooner had Ken gone off to arrange all this than one of the policemen came to the door to ask if someone on the hospital staff could go down to Thadipokhari right away to fetch reinforcements.

I sent someone else to find the nursing superintendent so we could discuss who should go. Not everyone on the staff was loyal, and of those who were, not all were free to go. Furthermore we needed to send someone forceful in case the police in Thadipokhari did not want to come. I suggested the hospital caretaker, who was not only loyal and forceful but also fast on his feet. Everyone agreed, so the caretaker was promptly dispatched with a letter from the policeman and told not to come back without help. We also told him to sneak down through the fields below the hospital until he was out of sight, lest the students spot him and, guessing where he was headed, try to stop him.

No sooner had I returned my attention to the patient's kidney than I heard the chanting begin, faint and far away at first, but growing louder and more distinct as the students drew nearer. The refrain—just one word repeated over and over—was unmistakable: *Maar-ne-chhau, maar-ne-chhau* (We-will-kill, we-will-kill). The chant was brisk and precise as if they meant business, but whom they wanted to kill was not clear.

Our minds were soon eased by one of our senior Nepali staff members. He informed us that the students were demonstrating against the teashop owners, not against us, and that they intended no harm to the hospital or its staff. All we had to do was keep quiet and stay out of the way and we would have nothing to fear.

I finished the operation to the chanting of the crowd and

went out to see for myself how matters stood. The open area in front of the hospital was filled with students, perhaps three hundred, lined up in regiment-like formation. Two hundred patients and their families, fifty staff members, and numerous other spectators, including most of the neighborhood children, crowded around the sides watching curiously. Many of the students carried sticks like toy rifles. All of this for the benefit of two shopkeepers who were accused of overcharging customers, most of whom were our patients. The two culprits stood in the doorways of their shops, ashen and shaking, listening as one student after another berated them for cheating the poor. The charges may have been partly true. It was well-known that some shopkeepers, often shamelessly, took advantage of the illiterate villagers. Perhaps the effect of the students' protest would be salutory; at the least, it was a relief to have someone else getting the heat.

It took the students two hours to exhaust their invective. Meanwhile some had become restless. They gradually broke ranks, formed into groups, and began disputing among themselves what to do next. We knew there was a radical group among them that was inclined to violence and had thus far been frustrated in its attempts to widen the scope of the demonstration. Whether this group would be able to stir up the assembly was a question that engaged our keenest interest.

Frenzied and conflicting rumors passed back and forth among bystanders. Two of our staff, previously "marked" by the students, beat a hasty exit—one into the X-ray darkroom and the other into a bathroom. (The purchasing officer had already gone into hiding.) The policemen looked nervously at their watches. Two and a half hours had passed since we had sent the caretaker to fetch reinforcements. It would be at least another hour before more police would arrive, this time with guns—our policeman had specified that in his letter.

Then the chanting began again. The students slowly got back into line. We awaited the worst. Then, still chanting, they headed back up the same trail they had come down three hours earlier. They spent the rest of the day demonstrating against the shopkeepers in the Amp Pipal bazaar, twenty minutes away.

With hearts thankful to God, we returned to finish the day's work. The patients who hadn't given up and gone home hurried back to the hospital to be examined. I went back to the operating room to sew up a young woman with a badly lacerated scalp who had arrived during the demonstration. Within ten minutes the area in front of the hospital was deserted; not a sign was left that anything out of the ordinary had taken place. There weren't even the usual patients milling about.

Into this tranquil scene a few minutes later trotted seven fully uniformed policemen carrying rifles, followed shortly by the exhausted caretaker—he had run both down and up. Seeing no one around, they came into the hospital and found me in the operating room. I was the only sign of violence they saw that day; I was covered with blood.

I left the operating room, still gowned and gloved, to talk to them. I wanted to show my appreciation for the tremendous effort they had expended. For a full two minutes none of them could speak, they were panting so hard. Their heavy khaki uniforms were drenched in sweat from collar to cuff, as if they had been caught in a downpour. They stood at attention, and their leader saluted me. Here, I thought, stood the pride of Nepal. Here was the will, the stamina, the discipline that made Nepal's Gurkha soldiers the finest and most feared fighting men in the world.

As soon as he caught his breath, the leader, still saluting, said simply, "We have come. What can we do for you?"

It was an awkward moment. What could I say? Sorry, we don't need you after all? Luckily the policeman who had sent for them appeared just then, so I left him to explain everything to the new arrivals. They received the information without changing expression; perhaps they were relieved that they wouldn't have to use their guns. The leader thanked me very much, saluted once more, and led his men out the door. They stopped five minutes for tea and then were off down the mountain. The whole affair reminded me of the little jingle about the king of France who marched up the hill with all his men and then marched down again—except these men hadn't marched up. They had run.

In the weeks following the demonstration, the general excitement continued at a high pitch. Rumors of new and greater demonstrations circulated continually. The villagers, outraged by the brazenness of the students and prodded by the victimized shopkeepers (who had been forced to close their shops until they cut their prices), sent one delegation after another to Gorkha demanding police protection and the restoration of law and order. The visit of the seven armed policemen, although unheralded at the time, proved to be an event of great significance in the minds of students and villagers alike. The students were angered at the "audacity" of the police but were also taken aback by it. Ordinary villagers, on the other hand, were emboldened by this show of government force and began opposing the students more openly. Even the pradhan panch personally led some of the delegations to Gorkha. The stage was set for a confrontation.

At the same time, we were having our own confrontation at the hospital. We caught our Communist bookkeeper, the chief troublemaker, in a small act of embezzlement and decided to fire him. We promised him we would tell no one of his wrongdoing if he left quietly, but if he attempted to retaliate or cause trouble for the hospital, we would report him to the police. We were taking a big risk. He was allied to the most radical, antigovernment elements in the district and would almost certainly try to get revenge indirectly through his friends.

It was a hectic time. I would do an operation, then run out to meet with the police, then hurry back in to set a fracture, then dash out to fire the bookkeeper, then hurry to the clinic to see some patients, then sneak out to meet a delegation demanding free medicine, then rush back for more surgery, then dash out to see an official from Gorkha, and so forth. To add to the confusion, Dom Bahadur, my chief surgical assistant, left without warning to go and plant trees in the Arabian desert. If only we could hold out for a month until the rains came. Then the number of patients would decline, and we'd have some breathing space. Furthermore school would be out, and the students would be scattered far and wide planting rice and thus harder to mobilize.

In the middle of the turmoil, the Chief District Officer arrived in Amp Pipal for a visit. He had received reports of the disturbances in our area and had come to investigate the situation himself. We had been warned of his visit, but he came a day earlier than expected. I was deep in the retroperitoneum removing another kidney stone when he arrived, so Helen entertained him at her house until I was free. He was a soft-spoken, courteous man. He assured us that matters were under control, that ever since the referendum the government had been gradually consolidating its power, and that they were getting ready to crack down on the students and round up the ringleaders. But, he added, it was still impossible to station police in Amp Pipal because he had none to spare. He would, however, order a "plainclothesman" to visit periodically to see that all was well. If trouble arose, we were to send word to Thadipokhari as before.

For several days after the Chief District Officer's visit all was quiet. On the third day, the plainclothesman arrived—in a bright plaid beret and pink shirt—to ask if we'd had any trouble or if we expected any. When I had nothing new to report, he concluded there were no problems, and after asking for a note to certify he had accomplished his mission, he was promptly off again on the trail to Thadipokhari.

The very next day we heard that the Communists had organized a plot to rob our business office in order to finance the purchase of arms. The report came from several reliable sources, so we felt the matter was of sufficient concern to ask again for police protection. In response to our request, a policeman arrived that same afternoon. After much persuasion, he agreed to stay several days. Even so, it was obvious that in the long run such protection was useless. We would be robbed the day the policeman left.

With this realization, we decided to hire a private security guard. He would be on duty from five in the evening until midnight. Then he would sleep on the floor in the narrow entryway to the business office, just beneath the safe, with a kukri by his side. I gave him my old army uniform from Vietnam (without the labels) to make him look like a real guard. Some of the missionary women were alarmed at the measure, but the men on the team prevailed.

We asked the policeman to please stay until our new guard could start work. He agreed, though reluctantly. His reluctance was understandable. The room we had given him to sleep in was infested with bedbugs. So we let him sleep in the prayer room. After several days, however, we learned that troublemaker number two on our staff (now number one since we had fired the bookkeeper) had also been sleeping in the prayer room. This relationship was too chummy for our liking. It was unsettling not to know on whose side the police were—we had enough trouble sorting out everyone else. So I told the staff member he could no longer sleep in the prayer room. That was all right with him, but that evening the policeman came to my house to say he was afraid to sleep alone. Couldn't his friend sleep with him as before? I granted his request. Then he showed me his flashlight and asked for two new batteries. I gave them. That night he would be happy and guard us well.

I hoped our new security guard would not be afraid to sleep alone. There was room for only one person under the safe.

Tila Kumari

I N SPITE OF THE OCCASIONAL DISASTER, faith in surgery has grown steadily over the years, and the volume of work has increased accordingly. Patients walk three to four days to obtain surgical consultation and treatment at our hospital. It's difficult not to be pleased and even proud about such a development.

One operation, especially, has become popular—the vaginal hysterectomy, for prolapse of the uterus. This is a distressing condition of women who have borne children. The uterus descends through the vagina and hangs down between the legs, sometimes reaching the size of a large melon. It is often covered with bleeding, purulent sores. The victim is not so incapacitated that she cannot perform her usual household chores, so the average husband has little incentive to incur the expense of an operation to cure her condition. If she can work, that is sufficient for him.

Through the generosity of some friends at home, a small fund was set up a few years ago to subsidize these operations, making it possible for us to offer the entire treatment free of charge. As a result, husbands began to bring their wives, and by the end of the first fund's first three years, we had operated successfully on forty-nine women.

The fiftieth patient to come for a vaginal hysterectomy was referred to us by the chief doctor of the government hospital in Gorkha. This woman, Tila Kumari, belonged to a prominent and wealthy family. Her husband was a banker, and her three sons all had respectable positions in the district government. Her daughter Soma, an assistant nurse at the government hospital, accompanied her mother and planned to stay with her throughout her hospitalization. She was an attractive and well-mannered girl, very devoted and attentive to her mother, as is usual among Nepalis, yet very apprehensive lest any danger or difficulty arise during her mother's treatment. Like a pitchman touting a new cure, I assured her we had had no complications from the operation so far and that it had been uniformly successful. The mother asked the usual questions: How long must I stay in the hospital? Will I be able to work after the operation? What can I eat after the operation? My answers apparently conformed to their preexisting notions, because they seemed reasonably satisfied. We admitted the mother to one of our two private rooms, along with Soma, who was to serve as her private duty nurse.

I performed the operation three days later. Soma asked if she could watch, and I was happy to oblige. All went smoothly, and Soma seemed impressed. She was particularly awed by the rows of shiny instruments provided by the U.S. Army.

She said, "It's sure much simpler having it done here than going all the way into Kathmandu."

During the operation I explained each step to Soma and answered all her questions. As her mother was wheeled out of the operating room, Soma said, "Thank you so much, doctor. My mother and I are very happy to have come here. You will be seeing her tonight, will you not?"

"Yes," I said, "I'll be by tonight." Then I went to the outpatient clinic where the usual crowd of patients was waiting impatiently to be seen.

The tranquility of Tila Kumari and her daughter was short-lived. No sooner had the spinal anesthetic worn off than the mother began to complain bitterly of pain, and the daughter began to worry that something had gone wrong. They were not reassured when told that pain was an inevitable, though temporary, consequence of any operation and not to worry.

During the night the nurse was called in to see the patient every few minutes. The next day brought only slight improvement. Nothing about the patient's condition was irregular except for her intense anxiety. I could not determine whether the mother or daughter was worrying the other more, but it was certainly clear that their effect on each other was synergistic.

For the next three days, our staff demonstrated surprising forbearance and understanding, especially since they were subject to considerable abuse for not attending promptly enough to the patient's needs. Other family members came to visit, each demanding to see the doctor to learn in detail about the patient's condition. Needless to say, the doctor's version and that of the mother and daughter correlated hardly at all. One relative was promptly dispatched to call for more relatives to come the following day, including the husband, who had not yet made an appearance. One son brought a letter from the government doctor asking for a report on the patient he had referred. And all during these first few days, the condition of the patient was completely unremarkable.

On the fourth postoperative day, the patient developed a fever. Soma launched herself into a new orbit of frenzy; the mother announced she was about to expire. A careful examination revealed no cause for the fever. I reassured the family, albeit this time more lamely.

The fever persisted. The patient's abdomen became distended, and she lost her appetite. Evidence of some inflammation at the operative site appeared, but not more than I had noted in a number of other similar cases. But for the first time, I became slightly worried. *How awful,* I thought, *if this woman, of all cases, has a complication or a prolonged hospital course.*

I had told Soma that her mother would be ready to go home on the seventh or eighth day after surgery. Now the seventh day had come. To minimize the family's worry, I tried to underplay my own concern and to treat the matter casually, as if things were going along pretty much as expected. Three or four times a day I told the family, and myself, that I fully anticipated the fever would be gone by the next day and that the patient would recover uneventfully.

The eighth postoperative day found the patient slightly improved and the fever reduced. I breathed a sigh of relief. I thought to myself that I needn't have gotten so worried—it was only because this was a special patient and because the reputation of our surgery was so much at stake. A lot of post-op patients have a fever for a few days, and I think little of it.

On the ninth day the patient's condition had further improved. For the first time since the operation, I looked forward to meeting Soma and whichever other relatives happened to be there that day. Tila Kumari no longer lamented that she was about to die. Instead she began to ask when she'd be able to go home.

"Within a couple of days now," I told her confidently. "You've been a little slower than usual to come around," as if, somehow, she had been responsible for the delay. I was already composing in my mind a letter to the government doctor explaining why her hospital stay had been prolonged, so he would not suspect that anything out of the ordinary had occurred.

By the tenth postoperative day, the fever had abated, and the patient and her daughter greeted me with smiling faces. I checked the operative site to make sure no inflammation remained. On examination the wound was still slightly thickened and tender, but since my previous examination several days earlier, it was much improved.

"Everything is coming along fine," I said. "You'll be ready to go home the day after tomorrow."

Half an hour later in the middle of the crowded outpatient waiting area, someone clutched my arm. It was Soma.

"My mother is having a terrible rigor, and her temperature is a hundred and four. Please come quickly."

I hurried back to her mother's room. Tila Kumari was indeed having a chill. Some bacteria and their toxins had evidently been released into the bloodstream as a result of my recent examination. Such chills almost always passed quickly; nevertheless, I was dismayed and alarmed that this had happened to a patient whom, only half an hour before, I had pronounced virtually healed.

Once more I tried to reassure the family. "It's nothing serious; it will pass. It's only from my examination. It happens from time to time."

A difficult operation was scheduled for that day, so I was many hours in the operating room. In the meantime my special patient's condition was dramatically and rapidly deteriorating, along with that of her daughter. The mother had become semiconscious; her fever out of control. Soma was hysterical, alternately screaming, weeping, and grabbing at anyone she thought could help or at least provide comfort.

When I finished in the operating room, I went straight to see Tila Kumari. As soon as I saw her, my heart sank. She was in critical condition—unresponsive, with a rapid, thready pulse and quick, shallow respirations. She was in septic shock, the final and most dreaded manifestation of infection. Once it appeared, it was often irreversible. No longer did I think with embarrassment of the few days' delay in my patient's recovery and of the need to act as if nothing serious had happened. The awful realization struck me with full force: this woman might actually succumb to that ultimate complication of surgery—death.

The relatives were beside themselves; more than usual happened to be present. Their weeping and shouting, questions and recriminations made it difficult to decide what medical measures to take. Intravenous fluids had to be started and new and potent drugs had to be administered immediately. Somehow the necessary things were done and there remained nothing to do but wait and watch and pray. The family had been difficult from the beginning, but they did not deserve this. They were a close-knit clan and were deeply grieved and shocked that this healthy woman they had brought to me had been reduced, at my hands, to this desperate state.

By evening Tila Kumari had rallied a little. Before going to bed, I went down to see her. Her room was quieter; most of the relatives had gone to nearby teashops to spend the night. I left word with the night nurse to call me if the patient's condition worsened.

It had been a hard two weeks. Never had we been so busy. At one point we had sixty-five patients packed into what was officially a forty-bed hospital. When we ran out of cots, we put them on benches. When we ran out of benches, we put them on straw mats. When we ran out of mats, they slept on the cement floor. Not only were we operating every day and seeing record numbers of outpatients, but our colleague Dr. Helen was on holiday. To add to the difficulty, this was the day the Nepali staff had chosen to go on strike. And throughout all this, Tila Kumari's family had been behaving as if she were the only patient in the hospital.

I saw little likelihood that I'd get through that night without being summoned. Either Cynthia or I had been called almost nightly for the previous two weeks, so we were hoping to catch some sleep soon. But not this night. At 2 A.M. came the familiar pounding on the back door. It was the night sweeper. As usual, Cynthia and I both woke up wondering which of us was needed. The call was obviously about my patient, so I went with the sweeper on the three-minute walk down the hill to the hospital.

Tila Kumari was near death. I wrote a few orders for additional medicines, but basically she was beyond my power to help. I wanted to pray with the family but felt impotent to do so. From the family's point of view, it was ridiculous to pray to God for help *now*. Where had He been before? Why hadn't He kept His doctor from getting this patient into such a mess in the first place?

Soma was feeling particularly vindictive.

"What kind of operation did you do that my mother should end up like this?" she asked reproachfully. Getting no response, she added, "If we had taken her to a proper hospital in Kathmandu, this never would have happened."

Still no response.

After a few more sallies directed primarily at me, she concluded with a bitter attack on our nursing staff, saying, "I have never seen such lousy nursing care anywhere in my life."

I could remain silent no longer. Three of our nurses were in the room with us: the regular night nurse and two Christian assistant nurses, who had volunteered to stay with the patient on their off-duty time. They had been Soma's classmates during their training.

Looking sternly at Soma, I said, "Stop speaking evil things that are not true. I have never known any patient that has received more love and concern and prayer than your mother. You should be ashamed to speak like that."

For one moment she stared at me. Then she burst into tears. She came over to me and caught hold of my shoulder. Sobbing uncontrollably, she begged my forgiveness.

"Is there anything you can do to save my mother?" she finally asked.

"No," I said. "Only God can save her."

"Then please pray now to your God to save her life."

The only other family member in the room was Soma's father. He had been standing quietly in a corner beyond the feeble glow of the kerosene lamp. I had hardly noticed him.

"Yes, please pray with us," he said.

So I prayed. Prayers don't usually slide easily off my tongue in the best of times, but fortunately that is not important to God. Even so, He must have winced a little at that prayer bumbled off in Nepali at two in the morning. My basic problem was that I had no assurance God would grant my request. I knew too well how great were the medical odds against it; my request was unreasonable. Yet I made it anyway, and earnestly, too. I mentioned something about the love of God being a reality even in such circumstances as these, but then immediately wondered how absurd that must have sounded to them. I prayed that whatever happened God would somehow make Himself known to this family and that He would vindicate His honor. I prayed much more, of which I have little recollection.

"Now it's in God's hands," I said, and turned and left the room.

The next morning Tila Kumari was much better. All the next day she continued to rally. We continued to pray for her with increasing faith and thanksgiving. The family stopped complaining and demanding; instead, they appeared grateful for everything we did. There was a heavier than usual load of outpatients that day, so we were kept quite busy in the clinic and I didn't see Tila Kumari except briefly at noontime. In the evening when I went to her room, she smiled and asked, "Am I going to be all right now?"

"Yes," I said, "you're going to be all right."

It had been a close call. Many would say that God miraculously had healed her. Even if some denied the miracle, they could not deny the healing. Just the thought of her death chapter sixteen

left me in a sweat. I could almost hear the word spreading up and down the flag-stoned streets of the district capital and from there fanning out all over the district: "Tila Kumari went to the mission hospital for a safe and simple operation and died." There hadn't been a surgical patient since my arrival whom I had wanted more to do well than Tila Kumari. But now God seemed to be saying to me, "This is my case, not yours. All your cases belong to me. Every one of them is mine. You are nothing but my assistant."

In the middle of the night I was awakened by a loud banging. With great foreboding, I groped for the flashlight, located my sandals, and went to the door. There was no one there. Just then I heard the banging above me—rats in the ceiling. Many times we had been awakened by rats and had stumbled to the door thinking we were being called to the hospital. But there was one difference tonight: I had never appreciated those rats before. This time I did.

Back to bed. Finally, back to sleep.

Then the real knocking came. This time there was no mistake. Full of despair, I went to the door. The night sweeper said my patient was very bad and to come quickly.

When I got to her room, I was greeted by sullen and angry stares. The room was filled with relatives. I couldn't imagine where they had all come from.

The patient was moribund. There was nothing left to do, nothing left to say. We all stood just staring at the bed, each preoccupied with his own thoughts.

Within an hour Tila Kumari was dead.

chapter seventeen

Maya Gurseni

*T*HE SMALL GROUP OF MEN moved carefully along the narrow, rocky path that led across the steep upper slopes of Liglig Mountain to the Amp Pipal Hospital. A large, dense cloud had gathered on the mountain, obscuring everything from view. It was dusk, the end of a steamy, rainy August day in the middle of the monsoons. The men had been walking two days. On the ridge ahead they could finally discern the electric lights of the hospital blinking faintly through the thick fog. Two of the men labored awkwardly and wearily under a long, heavy pole that they carried on their shoulders and from which was suspended a crude hammock. In the hammock lay a thirty-five-year-old woman, Maya Gurseni, in her sixth day of labor. Ahead on the path were her husband and his brother; behind came two alternate carriers to spell the first pair.

It was their first visit to the hospital. The husband had been been advised not to come, that the village witch doctors and priests knew what to do—provided sufficient money was offered for their services and suitable goats and chickens were properly sacrificed. But when his wife began to bleed "many handfuls" on the fourth day of labor, the husband decided not to listen further to his neighbors nor the village priests and elders. Maya Gurseni had borne him two daughters; two sons had died at birth. He wanted a son badly, but now he would be happy if only he could save his wife.

His decision to go to the hospital seemed rash. Nepalis did not reject lightly the local wisdom and tradition handed down over centuries. The priests threatened retribution not only on his wife but also on himself. His friends scoffed. Then, too, there was the problem of money. He would have to pay carriers four hundred rupees just to get his wife to the hospital, perhaps as much as the total hospital bill and certainly as much as a man could earn in two months of hard work, assuming he could find work and assuming he didn't have to spend every *pice* he earned for his daily rice, which was the usual case. And what would happen at that strange foreign hospital? A man from across the river had gone there and died the year before.

But he had decided to risk everything and go; and now here they were at the end of their journey. As they passed the generator shed, the roar of the motor reawakened some of their superstitious fears. Entering the hospital, they squinted at the unaccustomed brightness of the electric lights; except for the husband, none had ever seen a light bulb. However the familiar-looking faces of other patients and their relatives and the contented clucking of two chickens under a patient's bed in the main corridor reassured them that this was still Nepal.

The Nepali assistant nurse quickly determined that this new arrival was a *sutkeri* (delivery case) and led the party to the maternity ward. After examining the patient for a few minutes, she sent for the senior Nepali nurse on call. The senior nurse, after checking the patient, called our Norwegian nursing superintendent, Rigmor Hildershavn, who was always available for obstetric problems and could handle almost anything but a Caesarean section. About half an hour later, Rigmor emerged from the delivery room looking disconcerted and went to the vintage 1930-style phone and cranked out two longs and a short, our "number." (We have our own internal battery-run phone system that connects the hospital with the various mission houses.)

"I have an unusual case down here: a woman about to deliver, who has a tender abdomen and something the size of a grapefruit sitting on top of her uterus. She's pretty bad; she's been bleeding and she's as white as your shirt."

"I'll be right down," I said. I fetched my umbrella and was out the door.

The case was indeed unusual. The patient was in agony, and her entire abdomen was tender to touch. The "grapefruit" had become even more prominent. It was evident to me that the woman's uterus either had ruptured or was about to and that an emergency Caesarean section was necessary.

I found the husband waiting for us outside the delivery room. "We'll have to do an operation to take the baby out," I told him.

He didn't seem surprised. "Whatever you have to do, go ahead and do it," he said deliberately, as if he had long before made up his mind to accept the advice of the foreign hospital people.

"Good," I said. "We'll have to give her some blood."

"Blood?"

"Yes. We can't operate until we've given her at least two *manas* (pints) of blood."

"Two manas?" He figured that was about all the blood an average person had. A month earlier they had slit the throat of a big pig in his village and collected its blood in a basin—it had come to two manas.

"We only take one mana from any one person," I reassured him. I explained that the patient's family and friends should be willing to donate their blood first. Only if their blood was insufficient or didn't match the patient's would we ask some of our hospital staff to volunteer.

The husband's decision to follow whatever the doctor advised had not included giving a pint of his own blood.

"I can't possibly give my blood," he said in a voice noticeably feebler than before. "I'm weak myself. Besides, it's the planting season; I have to be able to work."

Meanwhile the man's brother and the four carriers had approached within a discreet distance and were listening intently. Relatives of other hospitalized patients had also drawn near, eager to give the new arrivals advice on any medical subject that might arise.

"I knew a man who gave blood and couldn't stand up for a month," offered one tall, sour Brahmin, the husband of a mental patient. Ever since his arrival some days earlier, he had been regarding everything done in the hospital with open disdain and suspicion.

"They'll take more than a mana," someone else predicted.

"Well, are you just going to let her die?" asked a young schoolteacher earnestly.

As the gathering increased, the contributions became more animated. Finally a middle-aged, slightly built man pushed his way forward and said with authority, "I just gave my blood a few days ago. Nothing happened to me; I'm as strong as ever."

The skeptics were silenced. The husband agreed, as well as his brother. We looked for the four carriers—the more donors we had, the likelihood that we would find one whose blood matched the patient's—but they were nowhere to be found. In fact we never saw them again. Giving blood had not been part of their contract.

Next we had to send for the necessary hospital staff. Since it was after seven in the evening, all our regular people had gone home. We called the lab man to do the cross-matching and draw the blood; he lived half an hour up the mountain. Three of the operating-room staff had to be summoned from varying distances. We usually sent the sweeper to do the fetching, since we had no other means of communication.

This particular night the sweeper on duty was our old friend Prem Bahadur, as steady as a rock and just as quick—and in vigorous health except for his night blindness.

At eight o'clock preparations in the operating room got under way with Prakash, our Christian anesthetist and the only one of the Nepali team members who lived near the hospital, supervising. Only six nights before, we had performed a Caesarean section on Prakash's wife for abruptio placenta. It was her first child, two months premature. The infant was unable to breathe on its own. Since Prakash was the most skilled among us in passing an endotracheal tube, he was asked to intubate his own child—a task he performed coolly, though with considerable difficulty. In spite of the combined efforts of Cynthia, Rigmor, and Prakash, the child eventually succumbed two hours after it was born. Yet there was little time to mourn in a country like Nepal; here was Prakash again tonight, hoping to spare another family the grief he had so recently experienced.

An hour after sending old Prem Bahadur out into the night, Lila Shrestha, the lab technician, arrived. Much depended on him because we could not proceed with the surgery until we gave the patient at least one blood transfusion. The patient's hemoglobin was forty percent of normal. So the husband and his brother, along with Cynthia, myself, and one or two other Nepali Christian staff members who were on duty, went to the lab to have our blood matched against Maya Gurseni's. This procedure would take another half-hour, so after giving our blood, Cynthia and I went home for a bite to eat.

In the lab, Lila began having troubles of his own. He had developed a high fever that day and was complaining of a throbbing pain in his liver. (Two days later he was admitted to the hospital with amoebic hepatitis.) Only the blood of the husband and brother matched. Unfortunately the husband passed out after only half a pint had been drawn. His brother, who had been watching as he awaited his turn, experienced an abrupt change of heart. Only by the most strenuous exhortations did we finally convince him to give *half* a mana and no more.

We needed more blood. At ten o'clock at night in Amp Pipal, blood donors are about as easy to find as date palms in Greenland. But Rigmor had an idea: Why not ask our six Nepali assistant nurses to give blood? They were living in the nurse's dormitory next to the hospital. Maybe they would be willing.

It seemed like a long shot. We had asked many times in the past if any of our staff would volunteer to give blood, but only a few had ever been willing, and of those, none had been girls. So we were all the more surprised and thankful when all six of the assistant nurses trooped sleepily into the hospital. They were all uncommonly plump for Nepali girls, and, as luck would have it, the two that matched were the chubbiest of all, with tiny little threadlike veins hidden under layers of adipose. By this time Lila could barely stand because of the pain in his liver; nevertheless, after gamely poking and jabbing the girls in various places he managed to extract from them almost half a pint each—enough, as it turned out, to allow us to complete the operation without mishap.

I cannot explain naturally why this patient survived her surgery. I believe an unseen hand stopped the bleeding from the huge, necrotic, hemorrhagic mass, permitting us to remove with minimal blood loss not only the fetus, which had died only a few hours earlier, but also the remains of the uterus. Maya Gurseni did not merely survive; she behaved as if she had never been operated on. She was up and about and eating two days later. Her temperature never rose above 98.6 degrees, and she was ready to leave the hospital on the eighth postoperative day. The only problem occurred when her husband could not find porters to carry her home. Porters were not readily available during the busy rice-planting season.

Furthermore a delivery case was considered "unclean," so no men other than close friends and relatives were willing to contaminate themselves by carrying such a patient—except at a very high price. As it was, the husband had spent almost all his savings on the first set of carriers. His wife's entire medical treatment, amounting to about forty dollars, was given free. So there was nothing for them to do but stay several days in one of the nearby teashops until she was strong enough to walk the long trail home. The journey would take her four days.

On several occasions preceding her discharge from the hospital, I told Maya Gurseni and her husband how the one great God had saved her life. Each time she would smile and say, "You are like a 'god' to us," using the word that signifies one of the many deities Nepalis worship. "You are our *bhagwaan*."

"No, I am only God's helper. It is God Himself you must thank."

But she could only repeat, "You are our bhagwaan." She seemed unable to comprehend the one true God above all other gods and remained content simply to add to her panoply of deities most of the staff of the Amp Pipal Hospital.

We will probably never see Maya Gurseni or her husband again. We can only pray that they saw something of the life of God in us, though they understood it not, and that some day they will come to know and worship Him. Or else, for what has she been spared?

Shaktaman Ghale

O NE OF THE FACES that watched with wonder as Maya Gurseni was carried into the hospital belonged to a twelve-year-old boy named Shaktaman Ghale. He had been admitted a month earlier, hollow-eyed and listless, with tuberculosis of his lungs and abdomen. After a mere two weeks of treatment, he had bounced back to life and had quickly become a favorite with the hospital staff because of his brightness and his good-natured curiosity.

His family was well-off by the standards of his village, Barpak, a two-day walk to the north of Amp Pipal. But they had come into hard times. Four months earlier Shaktaman's mother began coughing up blood. During fits of coughing, she would gasp and turn blue as the blood bubbled up within her lungs. In a community where most sickness was attributed to witches, no one doubted that a very frightening and powerful witch was expressing displeasure toward this family. Who was the witch? Why had this woman become the victim? To solve these riddles and dispel the witch's curse required the aid of the village's most influential (and expensive) *jhankri* (witch doctor).

After fifteen hundred rupees' (half a year's wages) worth of the *jhankri*'s services and no observable improvement in the mother, little Shaktaman also became ill with cough, fever, and a bloated belly. Confronted with this new challenge to his authority and reputation, the jhankri redoubled his efforts, as well as his demands on the family for more and bigger animals to sacrifice and new and elaborate rituals to perform. But to no avail. With death looming imminently for the mother and little Shaktaman getting worse each day, the father decided, in desperation, to try the foreign hospital in Amp Pipal—a three-day journey for one being carried. Maybe the god rumored to be at the foreign hospital was more powerful than this wretched witch. It was a small hope and so far away. The father knew of others from Barpak who, afflicted with this same disease, had made the trip to Amp Pipal only to succumb some months after returning home. He had no way of knowing the disease was tuberculosis and that they had died because they stopped taking their medicine.

The journey from Barpak to Amp Pipal in the rainy season is not to be undertaken lightly. It begins with a steep descent of thirty-five hundred feet where, for much of the way, the trail is simply an interminable series of slippery and irregular stone steps zigzagging down to the valley floor. Short stretches of slick mud relieve the monotony. Then for twelve miles the trail follows a winding, rushing river, passing from one side to the other at several points by means of precarious structures that might loosely be called bridges. One, called a *twing,* is no more than a stout rope by which the traveler, perched upon a tiny wooden seat, literally pulls himself across the swirling torrent far below. Then the trail leaves the river and climbs five thousand tortuous feet up and over a broad ridge and down the other side, then up again over another ridge and down, and finally the traveler arrives at the Amp Pipal Hospital.

In the hospital both Shaktaman and his mother progressed rapidly. The little boy's keen, inquiring eyes followed everything around him. He learned about his disease and then about other diseases. He learned of places in Nepal that he never knew existed, that were like strange and distant countries to a boy who had never been outside his own village. And the people that came from these places spoke differently, dressed differently, and worshiped Hindu gods of which he had never heard. Shaktaman's family were part Buddhist, part animist. They spoke Ghale, the predominant language of their village. Most of the people he met at the hospital spoke Nepali, but Shaktaman could understand them because he had learned Nepali in school. And then there were the foreigners with their white faces and funny mannerisms, always in a rush to go on to something else.

But Shaktaman and his mother were getting better—perhaps because of the foreigners' medicine, perhaps because of the foreigners' god, or perhaps simply because the witch hadn't wanted to make the arduous journey from Barpak to Amp Pipal.

Shaktaman had been in the hospital two and a half weeks when he started complaining of pain in his stomach. His abdomen began to swell again, and Cynthia, who was caring for him, asked me to see if his condition were something that required surgery. After examining the child, I thought not. Besides, the danger from a major operation in a person so debilitated would be very great. Before I would be willing to operate, I would have to be absolutely certain that surgery was necessary.

Such conservatism is usually wise in a place like Amp Pipal, but in this case it was not. For several days Shaktaman actually improved, thus confirming the apparent wisdom of my decision. But his recovery did not last. Two days after Maya Gurseni's operation, Shaktaman was suddenly stricken with intense abdominal pain. Shortly thereafter he went into shock from generalized peritonitis, a catastrophe invariably lethal unless corrected by surgery.

It was late Friday afternoon. The hospital staff was about to go off duty and wouldn't be back until Sunday. Shaktaman's father had left for Barpak the day before to bring more food for the family. He would not return for four days. If I was going to operate on this child, I would have to do it that night. And that was the question: should I operate or not? His chance for survival was close to zero either way. What would the father say if he returned to find that I had killed his son on the operating table? What effect would such news have on the people of Barpak? What would the other patients think? And what story would they take back to their villages? One operating room death in such a medically unsophisticated society could frighten away hundreds of patients with easily curable conditions. Wouldn't it be safer, even wiser, to let Shaktaman die?

I knew, however, that if I operated, Shaktaman had a tiny chance for survival, whereas if I did not operate, he had none. So I resorted to my usual method of escaping such dilemmas: I would present the facts to the family and let them decide. The family consisted only of Shaktaman and his mother. So I sent for the mother, still feeble and wasted from her own illness, though much improved.

I described to her as best I could her son's condition and his chances. As usual, I presented the situation in the bleakest terms possible, so not to raise false expectations. The mother nodded vacantly from time to time as if comprehending what I was saying. But when I asked her directly if she would permit me to operate, her reply was a blank gaze and some garbled words that sounded like, "Talk to my son; I don't speak Nepali."

She hadn't understood a thing. She spoke only Ghale. This should not have surprised me. Most women from remote villages of Nepal speak only their own local dialect. Only the men need to know Nepali, which is the language of commerce and politics—and medicine. I promptly sent the available hospital staff in every direction to look for anyone who could speak Ghale, but they found no one. As I pondered how to resolve this impasse, a small voice called to me out of the critical ward, "Doctor! Doctor! What are you trying to say to my mother? Please say it to me, and I will tell her."

So Shaktaman himself had to be the interpreter. The mother again repeated, "Tell my son; tell my son." Reluctantly I went into Shaktaman's room, sat down on the edge of his bed, and motioned for the mother to sit on a stool by the boy's head. They both had tears in their eyes as they looked first at each other and then at me. Shaktaman's expression was pained and frightened, but the alertness of his eyes remained. An intravenous solution was running; a large red rubber stomach tube emerged from one nostril, his breathing came in short gasps. He looked dried out, shriveled, except for his enormously distended abdomen. He seemed much younger than twelve.

"Shaktaman," I finally began, "your intestine has ruptured, and we are going to have to do an operation tonight to fix it."

He stared at me with wide eyes, as if by watching me closely he could better understand what I was saying. I repeated what I had said.

Without a flicker of emotion, he turned to his mother and repeated in Ghale what I had told him. As soon as he finished, she hid her face in her hands and began to sob quietly. Shaktaman fixed his gaze on me again, waiting for me to go on.

"The operation will be very dangerous," I said. "You might even die tonight or tomorrow."

Without blinking he translated for his mother, who immediately burst into tears and began to shake uncontrollably. Shaktaman spoke further with his mother in a rebuking tone, after which she gradually became quiet again.

There was a long silence. Then I said, "I'm afraid that there is very little hope that you will live. Perhaps only one chance in twenty—or thirty."

His eyes comprehended me perfectly. With earnestness, but with no more emotion than if he were interpreting for two foreign diplomats, he repeated this to his mother. When he finished, she looked at me with an expression of disbelief and reproach, as if to say: *We had so much faith in you; why have you allowed this to happen?* I felt more like an executioner than a deliverer.

I turned to Shaktaman and said, "Tell your mother I need her permission before I can operate."

I dreaded the prospect of operating on this child. I confess that I was secretly hoping the mother would either refuse permission or be unable to decide. There were good grounds for my hopes. It is most unusual in Nepal for women to make any important decisions on their own, much less a life-and-death decision involving the heir of the family. I waited, confidently anticipating a negative response.

Mother and son remained silent for some time, neither looking at the other. Then Shaktaman said, "My father has just gone home to bring more food. It would be good if we could wait for him to get back and then decide what to do."

"We can't wait," I said, trying my best to match the boy's detached and matter-of-fact tone. "You won't be alive when your father comes back. In fact if we don't do the operation tonight, you probably won't live past tomorrow."

"After the operation, how long will I have to stay in the hospital?" asked the boy, totally disregarding his mother's presence. She sat numbly watching the dark green fluid from her son's stomach gurgling through the drainage tubing into the suction bottle beneath the bed. "Will I be able to go home in a week—or two?"

Shaktaman was typical of patients all over the world who, faced with a grim prognosis, try to extract a more favorable verdict from the doctor by rephrasing their questions.

"Maybe in two weeks," I said. "But more likely three or four." Or six or eight, I could have added more truthfully.

After another long pause, Shaktaman said, "Is the operation very, very dangerous?" A slight tremor in his voice indicated that for the first time he had begun to realize that this whole discussion was about *himself*, about the doctor cutting open his very own stomach, about the possibility that he would never see his father or his home again.

"Yes," I said. "It is very, very dangerous."

He stared for some time at the ceiling above him, weighing the implications of what he had heard; a fleeting grimace gave witness to the excruciating pain he was suffering at every movement, at every cough, and even at every breath.

Then without another word to me, Shaktaman turned to his mother and for the next ten minutes spoke to her in Ghale. His speech was uneven because of his labored breathing, but otherwise his words came quickly and without hesitation. The sound of his voice was high-pitched and childlike, but his eyes and his manner bespoke the fact that he was now taking his father's place in the family council. I doubt that his mother said more than three sentences. When they had finished talking, Shaktaman turned once more to me and said simply, "My mother and I have decided that you should operate."

It was now my turn to stare at the ceiling. "Are you sure—I mean—even though you might die tonight from the operation?" I asked, unconsciously rephrasing my own question in the hope they might change their minds.

"Yes, we are sure."

I wished I had never raised the issue with them. I should have made the decision according to my own best judgment and not even mentioned the possibility of surgery. But there was no going back now.

Fortunately, I had asked the operating-room staff to stay late, so we were spared the usual preliminary routine of gathering them from the surrounding hillsides. Prakash was on hand to administer the ether, and within a short time, the team had everything ready. Two of the staff wheeled Shaktaman to the operating room.

On the way they passed Megh Nath, our recently employed Nepali purchasing officer, a young and enthusiastic Christian. When he learned the cause of the commotion and bustle, he asked if he could watch the operation since he'd never seen one. I told him this would be a bad one to watch and that he might better spend his time praying for the boy's recovery. Megh Nath replied that surely he could both watch and pray at the same time, so I agreed to let him observe the operation from the safe distance of the scrub room.

The staff lifted Shaktaman onto the operating table where he lay rigid and frightened, not daring to move lest he somehow betray his fear and disgrace his father's name. Then Prakash began to pray, as was his custom before each major surgical case, asking God to give wisdom to each member of the team and to protect the life of the small child He had given into our care. All the staff—Hindu, Buddhist, and Christian—joined their hearts in this simple prayer. We were ready to begin.

As always in dangerous cases, the greatest immediate risk was in the anesthesia. Prakash displayed the skill of an experienced professional, although he had only an eighth grade education and three months of informal training. He put Shaktaman to sleep smoothly.

Saraswati, four-foot-five and the mother of four children, served as both first assistant and scrub nurse. After she washed the abdomen, the two of us laid on the surgical drapes. Once the patient was covered and "out of sight," it was somehow easier to assume that dispassionate and calculating cast of mind that is essential for success in surgery. As I reached for the scalpel, I noticed Megh Nath peering eagerly from the scrub room. Prakash signaled that it was all right to proceed.

I made an eight-inch, midline incision through the skin and muscle layers of the abdomen. Then I gingerly cut a tiny opening in the peritoneum. Out spouted a thin stream of watery pus four feet in the air, just missing the operating lamp and descending in glistening droplets onto Saraswati's left shoulder and down her back.

"Quick, a kidney dish, a kidney dish!" I shouted at Saraswati, who was more intent on ducking the erratically shifting cascade than she was upon her business. Nor did our little geyser let up at once; in fact, it persisted unabated while we blundered about readying the suction apparatus. And the whole effect was enhanced by Prakash, who had kept the patient lightly anesthetized, thus causing the intraabdominal pressure to rise.

"Suction on! Suction on!" I roared at the circulating nurse, having difficulty making myself heard above the din of a sudden rainstorm that beat on the tin roof like a thousand elves beating on a thousand copper pots. "Suck! Suck! Suck!" I yelled, motioning vigorously to Saraswati, who was very hard of hearing even under the best of circumstances. Finally she managed to stick the suction tip into the hole in the peritoneum and thus put an end to the unexpected and unwanted eruption.

The entire performance lasted only ten seconds, but it was too much for Megh Nath. At the first glimpse of fluid shooting out of Shaktaman's belly, he had sunk down out of sight into a corner of the scrub room where he remained with his head in his arms until the end of the operation. In moments there were two liters of pus in the suction bottle, and Shaktaman was suddenly breathing easier, even under the anesthetic. I completed the remainder of the abdominal incision, as if the distraction afforded by the geyser had never occurred, and began the operation in earnest.

There were tuberculosis adhesions and pockets of pus everywhere. I had never seen an abdomen in such a terrible state. As I encountered each new abcess hidden between the matted loops of bowel, I left a trail of oozing raw surfaces from which bright blood trickled down to form dark pools in the lower portions of the abdomen. Very soon Prakash announced that the blood pressure had dropped to nothing. There was no way of cross-matching a blood donor at that hour. Besides, Lila, the only lab technician on hand, had been admitted to the hospital that same day with amoebic hepatitis.

We suddenly remembered that Dr. Helen Huston had arrived only an hour earlier from a week's holiday in Kathmandu; her blood was O-negative and could be given to anyone. Cross-matching was unnecessary. So without giving her a chance to recover from her eight-hour walk up the mountain, we summoned Helen to the hospital to have her blood drawn by Cynthia. Prakash had been unable to record a blood pressure for the past twenty minutes, and I had given Shaktaman up for lost. But when half a pint of Helen's blood had been administered, the pressure began to register again— first in the fifties, then sixty, then seventy.

But even as Helen's blood was running in, Shaktaman's blood was running out into the suction bottle. No matter how careful I was, the loss of blood continued. The pressure dropped again to sixty, then fifty. I could do nothing but pour in the plasma expander and intravenous saline and work as quickly as possible. Two hours later I finished the operation. All the while little Shaktaman's only hold on life was a threadlike pulse and Prakash's steady hand on the respirator bag. The boy's prospects were hopeless. I had no way to be sure all the pus had been removed, and even if it had, there was no way to keep it from reaccumulating. The whole effort had been a prolonged oblation to the muse of futility. And the only two possible outcomes were a slow demise or a rapid one. Tired and deflated, we closed the abdomen and wheeled the child, still barely alive, to the ward.

During the night, the muses changed. When I went to see Shaktaman the next morning, I was astonished to find him awake and alert. "I think I'm going to be all right now," he announced. I muttered that I thought so, too, which was a lie, and busied myself writing orders for the day.

"Am I supposed to be swollen up like this?" He lifted up the sheet to reveal his puffed up legs and a scrotum the size of a giant turnip.

"Yeah," I said casually. "That can happen after an operation like yours." This was true, if you add to it seven liters of intravenous saline in as many hours.

"When do you think I'll be ready to go home?"

I had become too absorbed in his chart to answer. I couldn't believe what I was seeing. His blood pressure had risen to normal during the night; his respirations were normal; his pulse was normal; his temperature was normal. After a moment's reflection, I shrugged it off. Desperately ill patients often appear to be doing quite well the day after surgery but then deteriorate rapidly thereafter. But this boy's spirit was something else. I patted him on the head. "Maybe in a couple of weeks," I said and walked out.

Had I the spiritual discernment, I would have known that

the new muse that came in the night was none other than the angel of the Lord. Shaktaman never faltered. Each day he grew stronger. One tube after another was removed, first the stomach tube, then the urinary catheter, finally the intravenous cutdown. Within four days he was walking about and eating with zest. We should not have been surprised. When the Lord heals, He heals completely. Shaktaman was simply progressing true to form.

One person was not surprised—Megh Nath. He had not fainted in the scrub room after all, nor had he gone to sleep. He had merely given up watching and started praying, which he continued to do until Shaktaman was out of the operating room. Others of our team had also prayed earnestly that night. And we can only wonder how many of our brothers and sisters around the world, with no awareness of the details, had been led that night to pray with us that God would magnify His name through our stumbling efforts in His little hospital at Amp Pipal.

Shaktaman's father arrived on the fourth day after surgery and appeared not at all perturbed that his son had had a "small" operation and was coming along nicely. He was pleased to contribute to the boy's progress by donating a pint of his own blood, declaring after he had given it, "Now I'm sure he'll get better."

Shaktaman and his mother were discharged about a month after his surgery and told to continue their tuberculosis medication at home. They had been patients at the hospital for a little over two months. The family returned to their village with an enlarged perception of the God who heals, who is more powerful than witches, more powerful than all the gods of Barpak. They knew that this God of the "foreign hospital" had come to their world of Nepal and touched them, had somehow even loved them—a behavior not associated with their own gods. They had heard about His Son who gives eternal life to those who believe and they were taking home a little book about Him. I cannot say that their new perception amounted to faith, but it was a beginning.

Even before they left, we were making plans to visit the family in Barpak some time in the future. When we asked Shaktaman how we could locate his house, he replied, "Just go to the big tree in the middle of town and ask anybody where Shaktaman lives. They will tell you."

chapter nineteen

Not Enough Money

I N A MISSION HOSPITAL most administrative problems come and go. But two come and *never* go: One is not enough money; the other is too much work. These two problems, over the years, have weighed upon us more than any others.

Not having enough money is nothing unique. Many organizations endure a chronic financial pinch tighter than that of mission hospitals. Consider government hospitals in developing countries or the governments themselves. The pinch comes when organizers undertake more responsibilities than they have money to support. No organization can responsibly spend money it does not have—not for long anyway—and mission hospitals are no exception.

But mission hospitals feel a double pinch. They do not intentionally choose to spend more money than is available; their situation demands it. The pressure on a mission hospital to provide service beyond its means is enormous. Mission hospitals are not found in wealthy suburbs; they are located in the poorest and neediest areas of the globe. The communities they serve cannot begin to support their own proper "full-service" hospitals. Thus mission hospitals are constantly either looking for outside help or scaling down their services—usually both. Looking for outside help is no problem, except for the time it takes. It is the scaling down of services in the face of ever-increasing need that creates the pinch—not in the pocketbook this time, but in the conscience.

For mission hospitals, being pinched for money creates more than the ordinary problems of having to economize and "do without"; it also creates dilemmas of conscience, for in the process of economizing and "doing without," patients suffer and even die.

The administrator of a mission hospital must often make choices in the interest of economy that he knows will deprive certain patients of life-saving treatment. At Amp Pipal, we have to let many resistant TB patients die because we cannot afford the expensive drugs they need. That is a choice *we* make, not the patient. We could write home and ask for money to buy these expensive drugs (and sometimes we do), but we are already writing home for money just to buy the ordinary inexpensive TB drugs and a lot more besides. Friends and churches at home provide the money for our TB-Leprosy Fund, our Powdered Milk Fund, our Disaster Relief Fund, our Building Fund. Money from home buys all our capital equipment; it sends all the missionaries to the field and then keeps them there; and, of course, it built the hospital in the first place. When all these gifts are added together—and this list is by no means complete—they come to almost a third of our annual budget. Our friends have been more than generous; it is up to us to use their money well, which usually means providing the greatest benefit to the greatest number. With rare exceptions, this rules out spending large sums to help only a few.

Hospital administrators in the West face similar choices, but much less frequently. And the choices concern far fewer patients, mainly those who are candidates for highly complicated and expensive forms of treatment. Not everyone, for example, can get an organ transplant on request nor even their blood dialyzed. Resources are limited, even in America. But on the mission field these hard choices bombard us daily. Not only do we have to say no to the exceptional patients, but to ordinary patients as well: cancer patients with limited hope of cure, the elderly and debilitated, patients with degenerative diseases, and many others, such as dog-bite victims. We do not stock rabies antiserum: Not only is it expensive, but the kind that is available is out of date in six months, which is how long it takes just to get here.

Many of the choices we have to make involve drugs, specifically whether to use those that are out of date. Most drugs are perfectly safe and effective for months beyond their expiration dates. Only gradually does their potency diminish. Do we throw them out? Of course not, especially when so much of a drug's shelf life has already elapsed by the time the drug gets to us. Most mission hospitals, in fact, rely on the free and cut-rate drugs provided by companies that are clearing their inventories. Many of these drugs are nearly out of date, but instead of being destroyed they are shipped to needy areas of the world. Not to use them would be absurd.

This all makes good sense, but the problem arises over where to draw the line. At some point an expired drug should be thrown out, but there is no way to know when that point has been reached. The temperament of the missionary doctor decides the matter as much as anything else.

I have always been reluctant to throw out expired drugs. I have more qualms about throwing them out than I do about giving them. And our patients certainly don't put up a fuss— they can't read the expiration dates.

I got stung once, however. We had just gotten in a large shipment of tetracycline eye ointment from the U.S.A. It had been a year en route by boat and was all out of date by the time it arrived. It was still ninety percent effective, we figured, so we decided to use it. Then one day the National Assembly representative from our district paid us a visit. His eye was inflamed, and he had come for some medicine. I prescribed the tetracycline eye ointment. Since it was late in the day, we invited him to spend the night. The next morning at breakfast he got out the little tube of eye ointment and showed me the expiration date, already six months past. (He knew English well; at one time he had been Nepal's ambassador to the United Nations.) If anything, he was more embarrassed than I; Asians rarely bring up unpleasantries in so direct a manner.

"Your Nepali pharmacist gave me this old medicine. I'm sure it's a mistake, but you ought to know about it so he doesn't do it again."

His diplomacy was typically Eastern: blame the pharmacist. I immediately leveled with my guest, not only to be honest but also to preserve the reputation of our Nepali staff. The staff was always being blamed by their own people for anything that went wrong, as if Westerners made no mistakes. Nepalis had little confidence in other Nepalis when it came to matters of Western technology, such as modern medicine. We considered it one of our most important duties to try to overcome this distrust by building up our staff in every possible way. We praised them in front of the patients. If we had to correct them, we tried to do it in private. Our intention was someday to hand the hospital over to Nepalis and let them run it; then they would need the full confidence of their countrymen.

"The pharmacist made no mistake," I said, and went on to explain to my visitor all about out-of-date medicines. I assured him that in six months his eye ointment had lost almost none of its potency. I also pointed out that we were selling it at half-price, which wasn't even enough to cover the shipping cost. Apparently I did not fully persuade him, because when I finished he asked for a different kind of eye ointment. I was thankful that he had not gotten a tube from the batch that was a *year* and six months out of date.

At one time we had shelves full of miscellaneous medicines that we had collected as gifts over the years. The only problem was that we could never remember what we had and whether it had been used up. Year after year the collection gathered dust and took up much needed shelf space. Some of the medicine was decidedly old-fashioned and lent to our pharmacy the air of an eighteenth-century apothecary shop. We had a hundred aged cans of foot powder, good for all kinds of foot conditions. We had a dozen bottles of Outgrow for ingrown toenails. We had a large quantity of Exlax—the first batch ever shipped to Asia, I think. Rats found it, though, and ate half of it. They then discharged its effects all over the pharmacy. When we finally discovered the problem, we threw it out.

Eventually we decided to clear out all the miscellaneous medicine. We dumped it into sacks and took it to the next team meeting, where we auctioned it off in mock seriousness to our fellow-missionaries. It was a delightful evening, more fun than we'd had in months.

Included in the variety of medicines we had accumulated were hundreds of ampules of Novocaine, a local anesthetic. Since we used this drug regularly, we decided not to auction it with the others. It was very old, but it seemed effective. We used it daily to pull teeth and lance boils, and the patients weren't complaining too much.

Then one day I got a toothache myself. I had broken a tooth several weeks earlier on a piece of rock in my rice and was hoping to get by without doing anything about it until the next HSB meetings. (The nearest dentist was in Kathmandu.) The toothache got worse, however, and I finally told Bal, my outpatient assistant, to pull the tooth and be done with it. I myself had taught Bal to pull teeth, although that did not give me great confidence since no one had ever taught me. (When it comes to learning new procedures, the saying goes, see one, do one, teach one. In Amp Pipal, we usually skip the first step.) So Bal injected some Novocaine, and started. After half a second, I stopped him and suggested he try more Novocaine, which he did. Half an hour and 15 milliliters of Novocaine later, the pain had diminished by about twenty-five percent, and Bal had gotten nowhere with my tooth except to break it off at gum level. His wrist was tired, he said. So I told him to call Bhakta, whom I had also taught to pull teeth, and for the next hour and a half the two cousins took turns trying to get the rest of my tooth out. They finally gave up, and I became the first and only dental-treatment failure in the history of the hospital. Fitting justice. And such pain! Next day I sneaked into the pharmacy and threw out all the old ampules of Novocaine.

Dr. Helen, who is as big and strong as Bal and Bhakta combined, pulled the tooth the following morning.

Missionaries, unlike Nepalis, usually won't settle for having their teeth pulled but have to have them drilled and filled and capped. At Amp Pipal, we don't fix teeth, we only pull them, so missionaries have to go to Kathmandu with their dental problems. I was happy, afterward, to have been an exception to the rule and to have been served with the same treatment we give our Nepali patients. The double standard we often use for treating Westerners has always troubled me; I wonder how much it has troubled the Nepalis.

There are many other ways to cut costs besides using old drugs. The medicines and general supplies we order on a regular basis are the cheapest available. We employ only the bare minimum of staff. We try to give the simplest and least expensive treatment possible, and then only for the more common and readily curable diseases (which make up ninety-eight percent of the diseases we see).

We look everywhere for ways to eliminate waste, breakage, and theft. Just about every item in use is controlled and counted, signed and countersigned—from sheets, blankets, and mattresses to syringes, soap, tape, and razor blades. We issue as few of each item at one time as is practical. We assess penalties for excessive loss and breakage of equipment.

The pharmacy is carefully monitored, and all drug usage is accounted for and recorded. The procedures in the business office and cashier's office are even more complicated.

We cut costs primarily to reduce the patient's bill, but it benefits the hospital, too. Many patients cannot pay the full amount of their bill anyway; therefore, lessening their bill in effect reduces the hospital's loss.

All these measures together have saved us thousands of rupees each year. But more important than controlling costs is controlling the doctors. Doctors are the single greatest controllable cause of high medical costs in a mission hospital—even though they are not paid for their services. Western doctors are not trained to apply principles of cost-effectiveness to medical practice; in fact, they have usually been taught exactly the opposite.

For example, in Western textbooks the treatment of typhoid fever calls for three weeks of chloramphenicol. But in ninety-five percent of cases, typhoid fever can be cured in half that time. So for the last ten days of treatment, the cost is an extra fifty percent for a benefit of five percent. In a situation where resources are limited, this reasoning can be carried one step further. Assuming a finite supply of chloramphenical, it is much better to treat one hundred patients with the short course and cure ninety-five of them than it is to treat fifty patients with the full course and leave the other fifty untreated.

This argument, although oversimplified (it does not take into account such issues as carrier states, for instance) can be repeated again and again for most of the diseases we see in Nepal. And it is applicable not only to the duration of treatment but also to the dosage at which drugs are pre-scribed. Doctors working in developing countries (and developed ones, too) need to recognize the economic implica-tions of their medical practice.

Western doctors and nurses are never taught the difference between "maximum" and "minimum" treatment. All training in the West is based on the maximum treatment. Anything less and the doctor winds up in a malpractice suit. In the hills of Nepal, there is no place for maximum treatment. Treat-ment at Amp Pipal is "adequate" for paying patients and "minimum" for nonpaying ones. Stated this way, our Western sensibilities are shocked. Why should the poor be discrimi-nated against, especially in Christian hospitals? The answer is: they are not being discriminated against. They are getting enough treatment to effect a cure—the minimum essential treatment.

At the same time, paying patients are not really getting a break. They are paying for their frills: X-rays and lab studies that are medically indicated but not absolutely necessary, standard instead of abbreviated courses of treatment, vitamin injections, admission to the hospital for convenience; the correction of minor burn contractures or moderately sized hydroceles (we don't do small ones), the removal of lumps and bumps, and so on. No mission hospital should finance frills for nonpaying patients, and the definition of "frill" should be broad indeed.

While mission hospitals should not be *losing* money

through unnecessary charity, there is no reason they should not be *earning* money from patients able to pay. Most patients expect to have their body fluids and discharges examined in the laboratory, and it is legitimate medical practice to do so; and it earns the hospital rupees. Most of our patients get at least one lab exam; it's like a tax. The hospital benefits greatly, and the financial pain to each patient is minimal. Some patients demand X-rays, and when it's compatible with good medical practice, we take their X-rays—and make a profit. Surgery generates income, especially for cosmetic and tranquility-enhancing procedures, and the price is set as high as the market will bear.

Setting a price on my surgery or on any other medical service is something I never thought I'd have to do as a missionary doctor. But mission hospitals run on money as well as faith. At least the money extracted from these poor people does not go into our own pockets, although some Nepalis find that hard to believe.

There are positive aspects to setting fees. Income from patients, after all, is what makes our medical services possible in the first place. Patients learn to value what they're getting if they have to pay for it, and they are also more likely to follow through with their treatment. When medicine is given free, patients often sell it instead of taking it themselves; they'd rather have the cash. Furthermore a mission hospital that is financially supported by the community it serves is more likely to continue to function after the foreigners leave; it has become in effect the community's hospital, and thus the people will have a greater incentive to maintain it.

Yet having said that, I don't know of a single missionary doctor or nurse who gets any satisfaction from charging patients. It's the most unpleasant part of our job. We'd stop in a minute if we knew of a better way to run our hospitals. Maybe there is. Let us know.

chapter twenty

Too Much Work

B *ESIDES NOT* having enough money, the other chronic administrative problem that has plagued us, especially in recent years, is too much work—that is, too many patients. If cutting corners to save money has led us into some professionally compromising situations, cutting corners to get through the daily workload has led us into some morally compromising ones.

In the early years of the hospital, we had the opposite problem: too few patients. Here we were with a nice roomy hospital and not enough work. Dr. Helen, who had founded the hospital, was away on furlough; a new staff was in charge, and patients were as leery of the unfamiliar faces as they were of the big, new, strange-looking building.

But things didn't stay that way for long. Helen had already done much to break down the prejudices against modern medicine that had been prevalent throughout the area. In one particularly dramatic instance before the hospital was built, she operated on a man who had fallen four days previously and ruptured his urethra. He arrived at the dispensary with his bladder blown up to his bellybutton. The man had been carried three days from a district that was only a one-day walk from Kathmandu. It was a testimony to Helen's reputation that he had come so far. The operation, carried out under exceedingly primitive conditions, was successful, and the patient recovered completely. Helen called it a miracle, pure and simple. (Ruptured urethras are not easy to operate on, even for experienced surgeons, and they rarely heal perfectly.) After that, patients in increasing numbers began coming to the hospital from that district, preferring to walk two or three days to Amp Pipal than to take an easy day's trip into Kathmandu.

Some years later a similar case occurred that involved a large district to the south. Not long afterward a new road was built connecting that district to our part of Nepal, which cut the traveling time to a day and a half. Now ten percent of our patients come from that district and from adjacent districts to the south, even though several good hospitals are located in their own area.

As the Amp Pipal Hospital's reputation spread and more and more patients started coming, the financial situation of the hospital began to improve. Patients may bring problems, but they also bring money, even if only a little. Our business manager, Ken Webster, was always telling us that hospitals were like department stores: the more customers, the more income. He should know because he used to manage a department store.

Up to a point, then, hospitals need patients. The problem is that the number of patients does not level off just because the hospital reaches its capacity. The obvious solution is to expand. In Nepal, that option is no longer open to us. The United Mission has decided not to expand its hospitals further. Instead, additional resources are to be put into community health programs. The decision is sound. We can treat most of the patients who come to our hospitals more quickly and cheaply in village clinics or health posts. Thus it makes sense to build up these smaller facilities and encourage patients to go to them instead of to the hospital. But at this stage, community health programs are actually increasing the pressure on the local hospital because more and more people are learning about their illnesses and coming to the hospital for treatment. For years to come, then, we can expect hospital workloads to continue to push upwards. And therein lies the problem.

Until recently at Amp Pipal, we have kept up with the increasing numbers through various unofficial forms of hospital expansion. We added whole rows of rooms for TB and leprosy patients, freeing up ward beds formerly occupied by these patients. We built a forty-bed (forty-straw-mat) "hotel" near the hospital for ambulatory patients. Previously when patients came for minor surgery or other outpatient treatment, they had no place to stay except in a regular hospital bed. (The local teashops, where outpatients usually stayed, were often full, especially in the busy seasons.) We called this kind of expansion "making full use of existing facilities," under which title we managed to get such projects approved by the HSB. Anything called "hospital expansion" would have been summarily rejected. We even built another eight-bed ward (a twenty percent increase in beds) right in the middle of the hospital; we called it "widening the ward corridor." That was truly "making full use of existing facilities." The beds were already in the corridor; all we needed was somewhere to walk! The widened corridor made life easier for the nurses, but it was not without price—we lost the flower garden that used to grow in its place.

But all these have been only temporizing measures. Our facilities now have been put to "full use," and there is no suitable space left for expansion. What, then, are the problems that arise when a mission hospital reaches its capacity, but the patient numbers continue increasing with no end in sight?

Some of the problems are obvious. A patient's time with

the doctor becomes less and less. As a result, things are missed, errors made. No doctor ever chooses to work under such conditions, but in a mission hospital, there is usually no choice. Oddly, this is more of a problem for the doctor than for the patient. The patient would much prefer to have two minutes with the doctor *today* than five minutes *tomorrow*—or no minutes at all.

In the ward, similar problems occur. It is so crowded, there is not sufficient time or space to give patients the nursing care they need. Mistakes multiply. Like doctors, nurses never choose to work under such conditions, but they have no choice if they are going to meet the greatest needs of the greatest number. Some missionary nurses have tried to run the ward the way wards are run back home: so many patients per nurse, so many feet between beds, and so forth. It's the ideal, to be sure, but to attain it means depriving too many patients of an urgently needed place in the hospital. Those doctors and nurses who advocate Western standards for mission hospitals are often confusing their own needs with the needs of their patients. It's very easy to do.

The problem of too much work is similar in some ways to the problem of not enough money. In the one case, we have to save money; in the other case, we have to save time and space. Either case means cutting corners and compromising our professional standards. But the problem of too much work leads to an even greater difficulty than the problem of money: what do you do when you *have* to turn patients away, patients who have nowhere else to go? How do you clear that with your conscience?

We have just begun facing this question at Amp Pipal. (Other mission hospitals have been facing it for years.) The logical place to begin is to turn away patients who come from areas that have their own hospitals. Patients ideally should go to the nearest medical facility.

The first patients we started turning away were those from the faraway districts in southern Nepal. They had no business coming to our hospital anyway, so some of us thought. Indeed, many did not. They were usually the wealthier Nepalis who could afford to travel and to shop around for the hospital they liked best. They were often snooty, refusing to see our Nepali health assistants and demanding to see a Western doctor. Their complaints were usually chronic and recurring—ulcer pain, headaches, painful joints—and not finding permanent relief elsewhere, they had come to see what we could offer. We might have taken pride in all these treatment failures flocking to us from other hospitals had it not been for the thought of our own treatment failures flocking in the opposite direction.

In our determination to turn these patients away, we overlooked the fact that the majority had come to us for good reason: they had not received adequate treatment from their local hospitals. Perhaps the doctor wasn't there, or didn't have time, or didn't have medicine. Some had suffered greatly and finally were coming to us in desperation.

I remember one pushy young man who came on one of our busier days. He was from southern Nepal. He had TB and had taken treatment for it off and on. He was now off treatment and was getting worse, so he came to Amp Pipal, his fourth hospital. I judged him an irresponsible individual, someone who didn't follow doctor's orders and who thought nothing of spreading his TB all over the countryside. He had refused to see our Nepali health assistants and had insisted on seeing me. He seemed like a good candidate to be sent back to his own hospital.

At first I said I wouldn't see him (I was in the operating room when he came), that he would have to be seen in the usual manner by one of the health assistants. Our health assistants carried a large share of the clinic load. Patients weren't guaranteed a doctor's examination. In fact half of our patients were treated entirely by the health assistants. Aside from the fact that the doctors didn't have time to see everyone, this was a legitimate way to discourage the hospital shoppers; if they didn't get to see a doctor, they probably wouldn't come back. Anyway why should such patients get special preference just because they were well-to-do and came from far away? Besides, our Nepali health assistants were first-rate, completely competent to handle most of the medical problems that came through the clinic. Government trained, they had worked with us under close supervision for over a year before being left on their own. Anything too hard for them they promptly referred to one of the doctors.

However the young man in question had told Sita, my office assistant, that he would wait all day if necessary, but he would not leave without seeing "Dr. Tom," as I was called.

So wait he did, and by the time I got to him, it was late in the afternoon. Neither of us, I dare say, was feeling favorably disposed toward the other.

After briefly listening to his complaints and looking at the X-rays he had brought with him, I told him he would have to go back to the government hospital in his district. I would give him a letter stating my findings, I said, but I wouldn't treat him.

"I won't go back to that hospital," he said. "The doctor there doesn't know what he's doing."

"Nonsense," I said, instinctively sticking up for a fellow-member of the medical fraternity. "You don't do what he says. That's why you don't get well."

"I've done exactly what he said. First, he gave me injections for a month. I got better for a while, then worse again. When I went back, he gave me some white pills and told me to take them for three months. I did that; I got better, but then got sick again. When I went back to him, he just gave me more of the same pills and told me to keep taking them. After that I didn't go back. Why should I? The pills weren't making me better."

I doubted his story. No doctor would treat TB with a month of injections alone, then three months of pills alone. Besides, patients are notorious for misremembering what their doctors say and do. (I've gotten the strangest reports from patients about what other doctors have done to them— even in America—and they almost never turn out to be true.)

"Then what did you do?" I asked.

He told me he had gone to two other hospitals and received treatment lasting one to two months each time, but nothing made him better. Finally he had come here to Amp Pipal.

Indeed, he looked sick. He was thin and dried out. His X-rays showed fairly advanced TB, probably resistant by this time.

"I'm sorry, you'll have to go back to your own hospital," I said. "I'll write you a letter to take."

"No, I won't go back there. Give me at least a month of medicine."

"That's the last thing you need," I said. "You need eighteen months of steady treatment with at least three drugs from one doctor. This skipping around from doctor to doctor is hopeless."

"I'll die before I go back to that hospital," he said, pressing his lips together.

He was being stubborn, proud. I still had other patients to see; I was running out of patience. More forcefully this time, I told him what kind of treatment he needed and why my giving him a a month's worth of medicine would do him more harm than good. I also said it wasn't practical to treat and follow-up TB patients who lived so far away; such patients rarely kept on with their treatment.

"But I've already come all this way," he persisted. "You can't send me away without treatment. Give me at least a month's medicine."

"No," I said, "and that's final." I was annoyed with him. I picked up the chart of the next patient.

The young man looked at me for a moment and realized I meant what I said. Then his eyes filled with tears.

I had expected his anger, but not this. The tears ran down his cheeks; it wasn't an act. Suddenly I saw that what I had interpreted as stubbornness and pride was actually fear. He was dying, and he knew it. And most likely he *would* die if he went back to that hospital. He had shown me the medicine the doctor there had given him; it was totally inadequate. If the young man's story was true, the doctor's conduct was indefensible. Or perhaps they had run out of medicine, a chronic problem at government hospitals.

In the end I did not treat him, mostly for the reasons I have already given. Moreover I still could not believe the doctor at that hospital was as bad as the patient said. I felt constrained to act as if I had confidence in the government health services. It was never our desire to outshine government hospitals, although many patients thought we did. On the contrary, we did everything possible—short of giving poor treatment ourselves—to build up the people's faith in their own health services.

After that I could never easily send patients away. I lost enthusiasm for our campaign to "limit" patients. I listened carefully when they told me why they had bypassed their own hospitals to come to Amp Pipal, and I gave them the benefit of the doubt. I could no longer worry about the problem of "outshining" government hospitals. We had a job to do, and our consciences demanded we do it well and with compassion. If patients came to us in preference to their own medical facilities, we were content to let the matter rest and give the credit to God.

One time another young man came from that same southern district, someone we ordinarily would have wanted to "turn away." He had a minor infection on his chin and had not gotten better at his local hospital, the usual story. He stayed a week while we treated his chin and became a Christian through contact with some of our staff. He went home to his village and soon two of his friends became Christians, too. Turning patients away is a tricky business. How can we be sure we are not turning away someone God Himself has sent?

The worst problem arising from too many patients and too great a workload is the tension it produces among members of a missionary team. Not everyone has an equal capacity for work. Furthermore some work is exciting, challenging, and interesting; other work is dull and routine. Some are accustomed to an eight-hour day; others are used to working until the job is done. A particularly difficult area is the relationship between doctors and nurses; doctors make decisions about patients, and nurses are stuck with those decisions. As the doctor's work increases, so does the nurse's, but she has no control over it. (Neither does the doctor, of course, but the nurse often doesn't see that.) Her wards fill with patients, for whom she must care, but it's the doctor that writes the orders and does the admitting and discharging. As a result, she feels threatened, used, and eventually resentful. She can't blame the patients; she can't blame God. But she can blame the doctor.

The doctor is caught between his responsibility to his patients and his responsibility to the nursing staff. In a mission hospital, there is no solution that satisfies everyone. In fact, in our experience, there's been no solution that has satisfied anyone.

In Amp Pipal matters came to a head some years back during a widespread dysentery epidemic. Our admissions suddenly increased ten percent. It was the hot, dry season. Water was scarce and springs were contaminated—a situation ideal for the spread of dysentery. The epidemic was severe: People were dying on the doorstep of the hospital, or within minutes of being admitted. Our I.V. maker was working overtime just to keep up with the intravenous fluids we were pouring into people's veins. The month was the busiest we had ever had. The Nepali staff rose to the occasion and performed admirably. In spite of the tremendous workload, they made fewer mistakes than I can ever remember, and they never did make that many mistakes. I recall being amazed and gratified. It's not the *amount* of work accomplished that primarily determines performance; it's the *attitude* of the worker.

But not everyone shared my positive view of that busy month. A few weeks later, our missionary nurses demanded we put an absolute ceiling on admitted patients. They would agree to fifty inpatients and no more, even though we had frequently gone over that number in the past. They said they could not give proper nursing care to any more than that. If an emergency came when we were full, we could admit the patient, but we would have to discharge someone else the very next day. We doctors reluctantly agreed to their demand, knowing that many patients would be ill-served. However we knew that if we did not agree, we risked splitting our team, in which case our service to everyone would suffer.

The demand of the nurses was especially difficult because, as it was, we never admitted a patient who didn't need to be in the hospital. Already we were refusing admission to many patients who ordinarily would have required it even by mission-hospital standards, to say nothing of Western standards. If our nurses had seen some of the patients we turned away—to keep *their* work down—they might have found it easier to accommodate those we admitted.

There was even pressure on us to limit the number of outpatients, though here the pressure was less since it was the doctors and health assistants who were mainly responsible for getting through the clinic each day. Setting a limit on clinic patients would have created more difficulties than it solved. How fast we finished the clinic depended largely on how many complicated and seriously ill patients came on any given day—which, of course, we could never predict. On some days, we saw over two hundred patients easily; on others, we had trouble seeing a hundred. To put off until tomorrow what we could finish today was to no one's advantage. Furthermore to ask patients to wait until the next day would mean that many would never be examined. Unable to wait, they would go home the same day. It seemed unethical to set arbitrary limits that would deprive patients of treatment even when we *had* the time and facilities to treat them.

A better solution was a time limit instead of a number limit. We would work until the staff had gone home. Even in recent years, we have rarely run over this limit. Almost all patients continue to get "one-day" service at Amp Pipal. With numbers still rising, however, this happy state will not last for long.

The problems of not enough money and too much work are with us to stay. And they will almost certainly get worse. We will need to find new and imaginative ways of dealing with them. But they must be ways that reflect the priorities of Nepalis who are sick, not those derived from the concepts and practices of our home countries. This is an injunction missionary doctors and nurses have all too often failed to observe.

God has called us to meet a need, of which our various medical projects meet only a small fraction. Thousands of sick people surround our hospitals and clinics, yet most we do not even see. And they are the poorest people. There is no way, given our present circumstances, for us to be able to reach out, help, and heal all of them. We have not the time, the money, nor the workers to do it.

But that is ultimately God's problem, not ours. For our part, we need to remain thankful for each opportunity God gives us to serve these Nepali people, even as they crowd around us in ever greater and greater numbers. We need to see God's sovereign hand at work increasing, apportioning, and controlling the volume of patients coming to our hospitals. We need to believe that He will provide the necessary strength to meet the demands He places on us, especially on busy days. He will not tax us beyond our (His) resources. Rather He wants to stretch us; it's the way we grow.

chapter twenty-one

An Abundant Life

O UR YEARS IN NEPAL have been the best of our lives, richly rewarding personally, professionally, and spiritually. We are content to be here; we have seen no greener grass. Adjusting to a foreign culture is as entertaining as it is enlightening, and the difficulties have made growth possible. Our association with a number of remarkable Christian colleagues has stimulated holiness and been a source of wisdom and encouragement. The medical work is a daily adventure in unusual problems and unorthodox solutions, and the opportunity to alleviate suffering in even a small measure brings its own reward. Therefore our predominant reaction is thankfulness to God, who has made these last twelve years possible.

Viewed objectively, little has been accomplished: two missionaries have learned an obscure foreign language and helped establish a small hospital on a small hill in a small kingdom where over half the people are too poor to come for treatment. An embryonic local church has seen a handful of Nepalis accept Christ over the past decade, during which time thousands of other handfuls have been born. These accomplishments are hardly worthy of acknowledgment, much less applause.

The Christian's standard response to this sort of gloominess is to say, "But God is working out His purpose." Skeptics will

immediately label this a cliché. And all too often they are right. We are quick to brush off a poor performance by saying, "Oh well, it's God who accomplishes things anyway, not man." The real issue, of course, is whether or not God is able to accomplish all He wants through each of us. As we look at the past twelve years with this in mind we must confess that our record is checkered.

Many assume that missionaries automatically and forever place themselves at the center of God's will when they decide to become missionaries. Far from it; that is but the first step. If they bungle all the succeeding steps, they might better have saved themselves the trouble of taking the first one. By far the most crucial prayer you can offer for any missionary is that he or she remain obedient and submitted to God, filled with His Spirit. When this prayer is fulfilled in the life of a missionary (or anyone else) it is not a cliché say that "God is working out His purpose."

God's immediate purpose is to communicate His love to people everywhere, and we believe that is why He sent us to Nepal. But though communicating love through medicine may discharge our responsibility as medical workers, it does little for the sick person coming for treatment if all he has to look forward to after recovery is a life of continuing unhappiness and hopelessness. The only way we know to help our Nepali friends in a lasting way is to put them in touch with the God who is the source of love and who sent His son Jesus into the world to demonstrate it.

We know from personal experience that God's love changes lives; the faith we share with our Nepali friends is not a hand-me-down or merely theoretical faith. His love changed our lives and sent us to Nepal; His love has kept us here. Many are attracted to Nepal by the spectacular mountains, the anticipation of adventure, the dramatic needs—and undoubtedly we were too—but such attractions will never keep people here. Only the love of Christ can do that. There are too many frustrations, too many insurmountable hurdles, for one to be able to carry on for long on one's own. Humanitarian motives are not enough. The humanitarian needs to be able to measure his accomplishments and see the fruit of his labor. But when there is little to show for his efforts, as is so often the case with work in developing countries, the humanitarian becomes discouraged and his idealism starts to fade. With us, however, the primary motive is to serve Christ. Thus, if our service to men is frustrated, rebuffed, or wiped away, we need not be disheartened. We are merely instruments to render *His* service. We share *His* love, not our own, and His love never runs dry.

What does Christ's love mean to us? To a Nepali? It means life, abundant life, that begins now and will never end. Jesus came that we "may have life, and have it to the full." And after 2000 years, His offer still stands.

It still stands for a young Nepali named Chandra Bahadur. In the fifth grade he was the brightest boy in his class. Then his father died. Since Chandra was the youngest son, he was expected, according to custom, to manage the household and take care of his aging mother. His older brothers had homes of their own that kept them occupied, so Chandra had no choice but to leave school and become a full-time village farmer.

One day Chandra went out to cut some leaves to feed his animals. Nepal has a particular species of tree whose leaves are especially savored by cows and goats, and which grows exceedingly tall. Nepalis are accustomed to climbing right to the top of this tree in order to strip off every last leaf-bearing twig.

Therefore it would not have been out of the ordinary to see Chandra perching himself on one of the highest limbs, hacking off the distal branches, and letting them drop to the ground below, except for one thing—Chandra had epilepsy. Once or twice a month for many years he suffered spells of momentary loss of consciousness, after which he would wake up slightly dazed and then be about his business again as if nothing had happened.

Chandra was hardly aware of his problem, and his family attributed the attacks to an evil spirit, the accepted explanation for epilepsy. On this fateful day, as Chandra leaned out along one of the highest limbs—perhaps sixty feet from the ground—without any warning he blacked out. When he came to he was lying at the foot of the tree with a stabbing pain in his back, unable to move his legs or even sit up. He had injured his spinal cord, an injury dreaded by Nepalis more than any other—for if a Nepali cannot walk, he does not survive.

Chandra was brought to the hospital the following day by a large contingent from his village led by one of his elder brothers. He had lost all neurological function below the waist and I realized immediately that there was almost no possibility of recovery. A slight, innocuous-looking angulation in his mid-thoracic spine at the level of the shoulder blades revealed the site of injury.

After our examination, we held a lengthy conference with Chandra's brother and the leading villagers. We asserted unequivocally that they could expect no improvement in his condition and that, under the circumstances, a prolonged period of hospitalization would be of no advantage. We had not yet seen a Nepali living in the hills survive this injury, and we frankly stated this to the family. No matter how much time we spent instructing those who were to care for the paralyzed patient, they simply could not adequately comprehend the exacting and unrelenting demands that their role required. Nor did they see the point of expending undue effort on a person who could not walk and who would never get well. As a result, bedsores inevitably developed, the bladder and kidneys became infected, the victim became demoralized, and within a few months died from inanition and sepsis.

After lengthy deliberation, the brother requested that we keep Chandra in the hospital for several weeks to see if by some remote chance he might begin to recover. After that time, if there was no improvement, they would take him home and do their best to care for him. The brother promised to bring food each day from his village and to provide someone to stay with Chandra in the hospital to prepare his meals and tend to his general needs.

After several days the person appointed to stay with Chandra had to leave; a few days later the relatives ceased bringing food. Chandra had shown no sign of improvement, and the members of his family apparently were hoping we would assume complete charge of him on a permanent basis. Soon people from his village stopped coming altogether. Although we sent messages to the brother, and on several occasions sent our hospital social worker in person, we received little response and no further commitment from the family or village members. We went as far as to appeal to our pradhan panch, hoping that he would be able to prevail upon the family to fulfill their responsibility by at least taking Chandra home—even if it was only to die.

While these negotiations were taking place, some of the hospital staff, including our South Indian social worker Annamma and our colleague Dr. Helen, got better acquainted with Chandra. Now that he had been abandoned by his friends and relatives, Chandra didn't want to go home. Although he had given up all hope of recovery, he wanted to remain in the hospital. This unusual reaction was prompted not only by his family's neglect, but also by the sustained concern and compassion demonstrated by some of the Christians on our staff. Although Chandra's prospects of recovery had diminished, their care for him had not. Consequently, after much prayerful consideration, we made the impractical and medically unjustifiable decision to maintain this paralyzed boy in the hospital indefinitely.

As the months wore on, every remaining flicker of hope for Chandra's recovery was extinguished. He entered long periods of despondency, sometimes longing to go home and die rather than linger on in such a useless and subhuman condition in a tiny cement-walled room, attended by people who might be gone in a year. He could see no reason to continue living. To make matters worse he developed bed-sores, in spite of our concerted effort to prevent them. The sores kept him from getting out in his wheelchair, thus adding to his general helplessness and immobility. As he became more and more depressed, he lost interest in food and even in visitors.

Then one day Chandra began reading a Nepali New Testament to pass the time. Something about it must have caught his attention, because for many weeks he was absorbed in that same volume, reading, pondering, wondering if perhaps there wasn't something in it that might make even his life worth living. Finally, more than a year after his injury, he stopped wondering and accepted Christ's offer of a full and abundant life—and found it to be real indeed.

I don't mean that Chandra rose up from his wheelchair and began to walk. Nor that has his life ever since has been characterized by a radiant and uninterrupted joy. What I do mean is that in a quiet and deliberate way Chandra Bahadur, once faced with a life that was without reason, found a hope and a purpose for his existence in Jesus Christ. He found an end to loneliness and an unfailing source of comfort—even as Jesus promised. In short, Chandra Bahadur became a new person: usually cheerful, often joyful, and always different from what he was before. And what he has found is so much greater than what he had that if you asked him today, he would tell you he is thankful he fell out of that tree.

Over the years Chandra's outward circumstances have changed. First he learned to type, and then to do the hospital accounts. He soon became one of the hospital cashiers, a job he continues to do. Financed by gifts from friends in Canada who were moved by his story, a special room was built for him off one end of the hospital. That room, though its dimensions are only ten by seven feet, has become a meeting place for staff, patients, visitors, and especially for Nepali Christians. Church meetings and prayer meetings are held there regularly. For the past five years Chandra has been chairman of the church committee, the governing body of our local congregation. He is an effective speaker and frequently leads the Saturday morning services, to which he is carried in his wheelchair. To the Hindu community, he is a continuing source of wonder—how a person unable to stand can even carry on, let alone become a leader of such stature and faith, is difficult for them to comprehend. For us too, Chandra is a continuing source of wonder.

Even the bedsores eventually stopped giving him trouble. For years following his injury he was unable to sit for more than an hour at a time in his wheelchair without opening up an old ulcer. We finally ordered a new kind of cushion from Canada, which was said to be effective in preventing bedsores. Since the cushion was expensive, we decided not to risk having it shipped; instead we waited until it could be hand-carried by someone traveling to Nepal.

Months went by and we heard nothing about the cushion. The church in the meantime planned an ambitious four-day conference, and since Chandra was chairman of the church committee, he was expected to play a major role in leading the meetings. But as the conference date approached, his bedsores began acting up worse than ever. We put him on strict bed rest and forbade him use of his wheelchair altogether. The sores slowly healed, but with the conference only a few days off it was still out of the question to let him attend. Even one hour in the wheelchair would open up the freshly healed ulcers and confine him to bed again for weeks. We met in his room with members of the church committee and prayed that somehow God would make it possible for Chandra to attend the conference. On the evening before the meetings were to begin, after nine months of waiting, the special cushion arrived. Chandra attended the entire conference and suffered no ill effect. In fact he has hardly been troubled with bedsores since—even working a regular eight-hour day.

Chandra could recall many other times when God has reached out and touched his life. And though God chose not to heal his paralysis, He has been Chandra's stay and support to a degree few others ever experience.

Indeed Chandra has come a long way since he fell from that tree. Back then he had plenty of reason to grasp for something—anything—a crutch by which to just keep living. But if ever there was a life not worth living, it was his. What crutch could have made a penniless Nepali boy, educated only to the fifth grade, abandoned by his family and friends to lead a degrading life with half a body, dependent on a foreign hospital of uncertain future—what crutch could have made him want to live? He needed something—and found something—that was great enough to make even his life worth living. Jesus said, "I have come that they may have life, and have it to the full." There is no way I can explain the change that took place in the life of this boy, except to say that Jesus is as good as His Word.

And that is the contention of this book.

afterword

Five Loaves and Two Fish

T HE HIMALAYAN FOOTHILLS have been inhabited for thousands of years. From what is known of other early civilizations and from what we can piece together from available historical records of the Himalayan area, we are presented with an unfolding story of men struggling to exist in the face of one adversity after another. In the two hundred years since the founding of the kingdom of Nepal, Western civilization has overcome most of mankind's natural adversaries and has entered an era of affluence unparalleled in history. During the same period, however, Nepal has remained essentially unchanged; most of its people carry on the same struggle for existence that their ancestors did before them. Life for the Nepali people continues to be characterized by an almost uninterrupted succession of toil, hunger, and sickness, only occasionally interspersed with the brief and simple joys without which life would be intolerable. Like the unending cycle of death and rebirth in which they feel caught, their life goes on, sustained only by the uncertain hope that next year's crop will be better than this year's, that tomorrow will bring less suffering and more happiness than today, that their next life will be easier than the present one.

But for the majority of Nepali people today, even that uncertain hope is dimmed. Something has happened in Nepal for which its history provides no precedent—something that

249

is creating upheavals in society and threatening to radically disrupt the whole pattern of its existence: the Nepali people have run out of land.

In 1920 the population of Nepal was approximately five million. Today it is over sixteen million. In the hill region, which comprises most of Nepal, less than twenty percent of the land is suitable for farming. Each arable acre must support an average of four people—the same man-to-land ratio as in Bangladesh, the most densely populated nation in the world. Even here the comparison works to Nepal's disadvantage, because the soil of Bangladesh is far more fertile and the climate more favorable than that found in the Himalayan foothills. The Nepali people have already filled their land beyond capacity, yet still their numbers grow. Within twenty-five years the same land will have to support double today's population. Since even now Nepal cannot produce enough food to feed its people, the coming scenario leaves little to speculation. Already, as a foretaste of what lies ahead, many hill communities around us have experienced recurring periods of famine, and in recent years, these periods have become more frequent and more prolonged.

Behind Nepal's romantic facade of peaceful villages, exotic temples, rhododendron forests, and the world's highest and most spectacular mountains, an ecologic and human catastrophe is inexorably taking shape, a catastrophe that will affect not only Nepal but the entire Indian subcontinent as well. As the population increases, the demand for farmland and firewood will intensify, thus accelerating the destruction of Nepal's once magnificent forests, thirty percent of which have been destroyed in the past decade alone. With less forest to hold the soil, erosion will increase, abetted by the steep mountainous terrain and torrential monsoon rains. In Nepal, where each cubic foot of soil is desperately needed, erosion assumes a frightening significance—the very basis of these people's lives is being swept in muddy torrents down the steep slopes into the Indian Ocean—a loss never to be regained.

The ramifications of this descending ecologic spiral are numerous. The disappearance of the forests results in reduced precipitation and threatens to transform Nepal into a semiarid wasteland, as well as to jeopardize the survival of millions of Indians who depend on a stable level of annual rainfall—a sequence of events already vividly enacted in the sub-Sahara region of Africa. As firewood becomes unavailable, animal manure that once fertilized the fields will be used for fuel. This will lead to a further drop in productivity. As the demand for food increases, steeper and steeper slopes will be cleared and terraced to provide additional farmland. When the yields decline, they will be abandoned to the mercy of the monsoon rains—more land to be washed away. The volume of eroded topsoil is so great that the beds of the rivers draining the Himalayas are rising six to twelve inches a year. This, in turn, causes these increasingly shallow rivers to overflow their banks, destroying additional large tracts of productive cropland.

Droughts, floods, and famines are well-known to the Nepali people; what is new is that after centuries of living in relative balance with their surroundings, that balance has finally been upset. A rapid and relentless deterioration of Nepal's environment is underway—a process almost impossible to arrest in view of Nepal's expanding population, which even now is beyond the means of control ordinarily available to non-totalitarian societies. During the past two decades, while the economic status of many of the world's people has improved, Nepal's per capita income and food production have decreased. In the past two years, even absolute food production has decreased. And the troubles are just beginning.

Let us for a moment extend our perspective beyond the confines of Nepal's boundaries. Nepal is simply a microcosm of the developing world today, and the process underway in that tiny Himalayan kingdom is mirrored with varying complexion in other countries of Asia, Africa, and Latin America, which together contain two thirds of the earth's population. Events of the past few years should convince Western nations that their own interests cannot be isolated from those of the rest of the world. The oil-producing nations have provided us with a conclusive demonstration of this truth. But as Christians, our concern for the world should not be based simply on material self-interest; it should arise from our responsibility to care for the needs of all men. And in this regard, never before have the demands on Christians been so great. And never before have the consequences of failing to respond been so momentous.

Why do I say "never before"? Let us imagine ourselves sitting in a classroom waiting to listen to a lecture on world history. The lecturer has drawn a graph on the blackboard. There is one unusual thing about the blackboard—it is six *miles* long. The lecturer has been plotting the curve of world population. Starting from the left, he has been six miles reaching a population of one billion in 1830. In six more *feet* he has reached two billion—1930. Two feet further, the line has risen to three billion—1960. In a little over a foot more—1980, the curve has reached four billion. And beyond that the curve will become even steeper.

The lecturer has drawn the logarithmic curve of population increase. It took thousands of years for the population of the earth to reach one billion. A mere one hundred and fifty years later, it has quadrupled. This is reason enough to say that "never before" have we seen such times as are coming upon us.

Let us now superimpose a second curve on the graph before us: the curve of world food production. This is represented by a wavy line, generally following the population curve, but sometimes falling below and sometimes rising above it, according to seasonal variations in the harvest. On the average, worldwide food production has kept pace with the number of people to be fed—until recently. For the first time in history, these two curves have begun to diverge. While population continues its increasingly steep upward climb, food production has gradually begun to level off.

Obviously the years ahead will be greatly affected by the degree to which these two lines can be brought together again. The outlook is not good. The prospects of reducing the rate of population growth within the next generation are very slim, especially if we rely on family planning programs as they are currently conducted. In fact the more the food production curve levels off and hunger-related mortality increases, the harder it will be to limit people's desire for children. Children constitute the social security system for most of the world's elderly inhabitants, not to mention the labor to till the fields and the means whereby a family's name and influence are perpetuated. Therefore, as infant mortality rises, the number of pregnancies will also rise. In areas where the child mortality rate is fifty percent, such as in rural Nepal, the number of pregnancies per family will generally be double that of an American family. If two-thirds of the children die, the number of pregnancies can be expected to rise accordingly. Therefore it is hardly correct to suppose that births can be limited by depriving people of food!

When we turn our attention to food production, the prospects for the future are not much brighter. To begin with, food already being produced is not reaching the people who need it. Even today there would be enough food to feed everyone on the planet an adequate diet if it weren't for three complicating factors: first, excessive consumption on the part of a few; second, existing political realities that interfere with the equitable distribution of food; and third, rats.

First, it is common medical knowledge that citizens of affluent countries are overeating themselves to death. When food consumption is measured in terms of dry grain, calculations show that the average Indian citizen consumes four hundred pounds of grain per year (which is almost sufficient); an American counterpart consumes two thousand pounds, much of it in the form of meat and beer. (Up to ten pounds of feed grain is required to produce one pound of steak.) This means that Americans consume between three and four times the amount they need. I believe that once we Western Christians understand that our long-taken-for-granted eating habits are ultimately depriving others of food and sending us to early graves, we will change those habits. And need we dwell on the billions of dollars spent each year to feed American pets?

The second and most important factor, world politics, is exceedingly complex, and thus correspondingly less under our control. Included here are such diverse considerations as the hoarding of food to raise prices—a common practice in many countries including Nepal, the loss of resources to the arms race, and the unfavorable trading position of the poorer nations. Perhaps even more significant is that so many of the world's farmers do not own the land they farm and so have little incentive to improve it.

The third factor is waste, for which rodents are primarily to blame. More than anyone else, it is rats that need birth control. Estimates show that in many areas half the food actually produced never reaches people's mouths; it is eaten by rats. Yet exterminating rodents is easier said than done, as anyone knows who has tried it. Provide enough rice, and an energetic mother and father rat will end up with five thousand progeny at the end of a year. Keeping ahead of such prolific creatures is not easy.

If there are a discouraging number of circumstances that prevent the world's potential food supply from being properly utilized, conversely there is the reasonable expectation that food production can be substantially increased in this generation. Few will claim that it will keep abreast of the population, but neither is it likely to lag as far behind as the pessimists predict. Nevertheless this optimism must be tempered by the knowledge that such a rate of increase cannot be sustained indefinitely; enhancing food production can only be a temporary solution.

It has been calculated that under *ideal* conditions, food production in Bangladesh could be tripled using the technology already available. (Presumably a similar figure might apply to Nepal and elsewhere.) These conditions presuppose the absence of all the inhibiting factors mentioned previously and the availability of economic resources that do not exist for most developing nations. Thus the outcome of man's struggle to feed himself in the coming years will depend in large measure on the extent to which he can translate the theoretically possible into reality. Herein lies the challenge that faces us today.

Two pitfalls need to be avoided at this point. The first is excessive reliance on technology. Christians are not likely to make this error, for they know full well that the root cause of hunger and suffering lies in man's selfishness and in his disobedience to the commands of God. More than we need a new kind of technology, we need a new kind of man in the world today—and this need can be met only in Jesus Christ.

The second pitfall to be avoided is an excessive preoccupation with the sin of the world. We find it comfortable to sit back, fold our arms, and mutter to one another, "All they have to do is to repent." But is that what Christ did when He rose from where He was and, with unfolded arms, came into the world to minister to us? Taking Christ's example, we need to minister to the world in every way we can. Each Christian, before God, must find out where his or her duty lies. To God alone we will be accountable. Some of us can start by reducing our consumption of meat, giving up pets, and relinquishing our "right" to a large family. Many of us will be called to a simpler lifestyle, to give more of our time and our resources—and still more.

We need to be willing to weigh our cherished stained-glass windows and church music programs in the balance against the demands of an effective witness to a watching world. We need to send some of our young people into agricultural research, and others out to apply what has been learned. We need someone to discover a practical way to cook rice without burning firewood or manure for fuel. We need Christian politicians to fight injustice in the world's political systems and to set an example of compassionate and upright leadership for all to follow.

And the watchword for us all, no matter where God leads us, will be "love." Love is the one quality the world can discern that sets Christians apart and makes Christianity distinct from every other religion. If we fail to act on this truth, we will lose our right to be heard and will enter the post-Christian era for good.

What is our own personal role to be as we face the travail of the coming years? The problems of overpopulation and hunger, already upon us, are too great even for governments to handle, let alone individual Christians. It is one thing to minister to a handful of hungry Nepalis at our door by giving them food, money, seeds, or a job, but when individuals become multitudes, what will we do?

Clearly our efforts to find new solutions will continue. If of little value for the present generation, they may eventually benefit a wiser and more sober human race. Yet the inability of technology to invest human life with an ultimate meaning and purpose should in these days, more than ever, cause us to look to God and to see our role from His perspective. When we do this, we not only find renewed vitality for the tasks at hand, but more important, we begin to see our way through the hungry multitudes pressing at our doorstep. For it seems that God is telling us simply to share with them whatever we have, and when it runs low, to try to get more, and when there is no more, to leave the issue to Him. He is telling us to enter into their suffering without concern for the outcome. He is reminding us that, as much as we have done for the least of these our brethren, we have done unto Him. We cannot, as some do, restrict the interpretation of "brethren" to mean fellow-Christians alone. We wince when we hear Christians refer to much of the agony of mankind as the judgment of God; it may be, but it is not for us to say or even to think.

There are moments when we long for Christ to come again and feed the multitudes, not five thousand only, but fifty thousand, even fifty million. He could do it. Those first disciples had only two fish and a few loaves, but they gave Him all they had. Is this not His word to us today—to give Him all our loaves and fishes, to give Him everything we have? Then, who can say what He would be able to accomplish in our time through us?